ELN

A Profile of Ejército de Liberación Nacional

by

K.J. Wetherholt

MIPJ

Media, Information, International Relations
and Humanitarian Affairs

Table of Contents

Preface

I completed the first version of this manuscript in April 2019 after four years of research, including in the field. Even as I finished that draft, the public trajectory of the ELN had shifted. The issue: the ELN has often been the less-researched guerrilla group involved in Colombia's civil war, less often appearing in the international press. This is despite the ELN having been formed before FARC/FARC-EP following the period known as *La Violencia* in Colombia, also following the Cuban Revolution, from which the ELN derived its inspiration. FARC, having originated from the organized Communist movements supported by the then Soviet Union until the end of the Cold War, by far, has received most of the attention; this was especially true upon the declaration of peace with FARC in 2016 and the beginning of its formal and monitored Disarmament, Demobilization, and Reintegration (DDR) process in Colombia, despite a referendum indicating the slight majority of the Colombian public—with a long memory of war, displacement, and violence—did not favor a peace that came with what they considered too large a degree of impunity among former FARC combatants. Indeed, so prevalent was FARC in the media and public consciousness that when peace was declared following the Colombian government under Juan Miguel Santos ostensibly setting aside the referendum, both the media and many in international policy erroneously declared both an end to the civil war—and if not more egregiously—that there was now "peace in Colombia."

This, as I suspected, would continue to allow the ELN, in remaining somewhat under the radar, to maneuver itself into a more powerful position using the cover of the peace process with FARC to expand its territory, its alliances, and its membership. The myopic nature to focus on what seems to be the most powerful group often leaves what seem to be "ancillary" or "less important" groups in the periphery. While it's natural to focus on certain non-state armed groups that seem to have the most power in order to negotiate a peace, or at least some kind of understanding, it often comes at the cost of ignoring nuances that in the longer-term will end up being every bit as important in the ever-changing landscape of national, regional, and international security.

One of the lessons I hope will become evident in reading this book: one cannot afford to ignore the "outliers" and underestimate their resolve, especially if they similarly have been in existence for a similar—if not longer—period of time. That longevity exists for a reason—the capacity to make decisions and adapt when it is necessary, not just for survival, but also for advantage when it senses a weakness or vulnerability in the more immediate focus among major stakeholders. This is, essentially, a basic tenet—and strategy—involved in the very definitions of the kind of warfare the ELN conducts: guerrilla warfare that against the state is inherently considered, in today's parlance (depending upon whom you're speaking with), asymmetric, low-intensity, and/or 4th Gen, when faced with the capacities of the larger state as stakeholder and/or target. The ELN, unlike FARC, has also still managed to keep, despite contradictory action among certain younger *frente* leaders, its philosophical and political message— grounded in liberation theology and agrarian reform steeped in Marxism—intact, at least among its overarching command structure, among whom it is still the pillar of their philosophy.

The ELN, as of this writing, has a major presence not just in Colombia, actively taking former FARC territory following the negotiated (and now failing) peace with FARC, in some cases forming alliances with dissident leaders from FARC who were not in favor of the peace agreement with the Colombian government. Importantly, ELN is now a presence in at least half of 24 provinces of Venezuela, operating with the assent, if not support, of Venezuelan President Maduro and the criminal *colectivos*, while also often controlling the illicit routes between the two countries. Like in the areas of Colombia where the ELN has a strong presence, in Venezuela,the ELN is taking on the roles of the state, ostensibly being a quasi-state presence distributing food, supplies, and acting as a security apparatus for the areas under its auspices.

This is the microcosm; the macro view has this coinciding with the interests in Venezuela by both Russia and China and the warnings about such a presence by the United States. Russia offers Maduro direct support, including financially, and now, most recently, with the presence of the Russian military. China, as it has in other parts of the world, offers billions of dollars in loan guarantees and other inducements, including arms and infrastructure, for resources. While the United States, generationally entrenched in Colombia including with vast multinational business interests, economic aid, and security support under Plan Colombia and other agreements, is, as it was a generation ago, poised to counter the Russian and Chinese presence.

While I hesitate to project a worst-case scenario, in this book I will offer a warning regarding entering into any kind of heightened proxy engagement should Colombia's trajectory continue to head down the path of instability, triggering any national interests the U.S. might choose engage with greater force. This includes neighboring Venezuela being in its own destructive chaos, aided by Russia, China, Iran, and its proxies. As the proud daughter, great-granddaughter, etc., of U.S. military veterans since before the United States evenexisted formally, my loyalties include issuing a caution toward any such kind of engagement. As has been suggested by many former members of the U.S. military, as well as those in policy, the "corporatization" of the U.S. military, including any potential re-invigoration of the Monroe Doctrine in the 21st Century by future administrations, has made it less likely to be prepared for the profound demands of this kind of engagement, with its roots reaching back to the colonial age and the independence achieved by Simon Bolivar. My hope is that we would have learned from now multiple instances of intervention, if not attempted nation-building, in the developing world. This is not just seen by communities in such countries as blatant imperialism, but with the additional development interests during/following any attempted peace, a continued and insidious neo-colonial mindset. We continue to learn we do not do as well in wars in which we have a lack of cultural and historical understanding, both in terms of the people involved and the stakes. This includes the arcane suggestion that sheer might on a macro level wins the day. Nuances matter, and this is especially true when guerrilla forces, active for decades and only growing in number and power against their respective states, know both the physical and human terrain better than any outsider possibly could. And as is true in any civil war, those combatants for whom the land is home have a greater interest, including blood stakes, in the outcome of any engagement than do outsiders who believe the status, sheer might, and technology of a developed state should make involvement a cake walk. This has been proven foolhardy in the past, and it lends, in moments, both intentional or unintentional hubris to the proceedings.

On a last and personal note regarding this book's scope and having been immersed in the rural realities of

Colombiano/as y Campesinos, having seen the effects and impact of decades of civil war, violence, and instability—with both old and new threats both ubiquitous and wholly visceral among them—firsthand, it took me another two years to finally complete this book's final version. It wasn't just because of new developments; the ELN, outside of the announcement of his retirement by its longtime leader, *nom de guerre* "Gambino" earlier this year, has only expanded its reach competing and/or collaborating with FARC dissidents and BACRIM (narco-criminal gangs) with little international attention; my experiences made me need to take the time to truly decompress and know what needed to be said, including as a neo-populist presence reared its head across the Western Hemisphere. Add that to a global pandemic and deaths of those whom I was close to, including two of them in the field, and I, like others, needed to take a moment to breathe and reboot before finally ending this chapter—both personal and professional. Those whom I came to know, and whose nation's history and current trajectory continue to come with unimaginable and often violent complexities, are still being affected by trenchant insecurity and an almost endemic cynicism about any true peace—claimed, adjudicated, or attempted.

This book, heart and soul, is for them, hopefully helping to illuminate some under-reported history that adds to their—and Colombia's—complexity.

K.J. Wetherholt

July 31, 2021

Introduction

According to Rachel Kleinfeld and Robert Mulligan in an 18 March, 2019 article for the Carnegie Endowment for International Peace, "the world is less violent today than at virtually any other time in human history" although "civil-war deaths have ticked up in recent years, they have still fallen dramatically since the end of the Cold War".[1] They also, however, acknowledge violence is "on the rise," including "state violence against citizens and criminal violence from mafias, drug cartels, and gangs" while "[c]omplicating matters, state and criminal killings are often intertwined".[2] And, last but not least: "According to the International Committee of the Red Cross, roughly half of today's wars involve three and nine groups…a mashup of local militia, criminal gangs, foreign fighters, and terrorist organizations, defying traditional diplomatic response."[3]

This seemingly contradictory series of facts—the juxtaposition of the world being "less violent" while "civil war deaths have ticked up over the years," including among "intertwined" state and criminal groups—as, according to the article, "one in six people worldwide [is] affected by global violence"[4]—only suggests that at least for certain areas of the world, not much has actually changed. One of these is the Republic of Colombia. Having spent time there in the field, while doing the research for this examination of the ELN, the actual experience of being in the rural areas among the rural contingents, or *Campesinos,* those whom

---

[1] Kleinfeld, Rachel, and Robert Muggah. "The State of War." Carnegie Endowment for International Peace. Last modified March 18, 2019. https://carnegieendowment.org/2019/03/18/state-of-war-pub-78630.
[2] Ibid..
[3] Ibid..
[4] Ibid..

Marxists and Maoists would have considered "agrarian peasants," made an indelible impact; being able to experience what many in policy or academia might not have made a profound difference in understanding the stakes, and how culture and socio-economic issues become deeply personalized. This includes the actions (or non-action) of the State when it comes to the concerns of those who are not powerful enough, in and of themselves, to make their voices heard, especially where corruption, power jockeying, and illicit activity run rampant. The pride of the Colombian people is intense; however, so is the conflict that has been wrought among them.

The late Virginia "Ginny" Bouvier, a Colombia subject matter expert (SME) and the editor of a book on Colombia, *Building Peace in a Time of War* (2009) for the United States Institute of Peace (USIP), in her chapter introducing the book, recounts her experience when she asked an audience to suggest all of the "words and images they associate with Colombia."[5] Her audience had no trouble coming up with such words as "war," "violence," drugs," "kidnapping," "FARC," "arms," "paramilitaries," "child soldiers," "corruption," etc..[6] As she suggested, "Colombia receives relatively little attention from the American media, the public, or the broader global community; when it does appear in the news, drugs and violence frequently dominate the headlines".[7]

Despite the book being published in 2009, with much having happened since then, these are still the kinds of terms popular culture might inherently associate with Colombia and its current reality; Bouvier's statistics regarding Colombia being "infamous as a leader in the drug trade," it

---

[5] Bouvier, Virginia M. *Colombia: Building Peace in a Time of War*. US Institute of Peace Press, 2009, p. 3.
[6] Ibid..
[7] Ibid..

was then—and still is—similarly a "leader in statistics on violence."[8] Colombia has also long been the world leader on internally displaced (IDP); according to the CIA, since 1985, and by 2018, there have been 7,816,472 displaced by armed violence, with 300,000 more projected each year.[9] This does not take into account the IDP's before 1985, which encompassed some of the worst violence Colombia had known in its modern history, including the period known as *La Violencia* (1948-66).[10]

Bouvier also points out the vast funding Colombia has received from the United States via Plan Colombia; as of the book's publication in 2009, it had amounted to more than US$5 billion, of which "more than three quarters went to the Colombian military and police for counterinsurgency and antinarcotics operations and oil pipeline protection."[11] According to the Congressional Research Service, between FY2000-2016, the U.S. Government allocated US$10 billion for Plan Colombia, with US$391.3 million for 2018 to help assist "the peace and end conflict."[12] This included, specifically, to help facilitate peace with Fuerzas Armadas Revolucionarias de Colombia (FARC), the largest of Colombia's non-state guerrilla combatants.[13] This included also fostering infrastructure projects in former FARC

---

[8] Ibid., p. 4.
[9] "Field Listing :: Refugees and Internally Displaced Persons — The World Factbook." Welcome to the CIA Web Site — Central Intelligence Agency. Accessed April 8, 2019. https://www.cia.gov/library/publications/the-world-factbook/fields/327.html.
[10] Manwaring, Max G. "Nonstate Actors in Colombia: Threat and Response." Strategic Studies Institute (SSI) | US Army War College. Accessed April 8, 2019. https://ssi.armywarcollege.edu/pubs/display.cfm?pubID=16.
[11] Bouvier, p.5.
[12] "Colombia: Background and U.S. Relations." Congressional Research Service. Last modified February 8, 2019. https://fas.org/sgp/crs/row/R43813.pdf.
[13] Ibid..

territory, such as paved roads in former FARC strongholds.[14] Two of the reasons for such vast U.S. investment: both the "War on Drugs" and the face that the U.S. has long had a presence in Colombia not just in terms of oil (hence the interest in safeguarding the pipelines from guerrilla and terrorist activity), but via other multi-national conglomerates such as Coca-Cola, Dole, Philip Morris, and such manufacturers as Bell Helicopter and Sikorsky (known for their Black Hawk helicopters).[15] Because of such interests in terms of both stemming the drug trade and protecting its business interests, the U.S. Embassy in Bogota had, at least in 2009, over 2,000 employees among 32 different agencies.[16]

As mentioned in the Preface, found in the Congressional Research Service's content, also represented by Bouvier's question to her audience, as well as all of the media attention that Colombia does receive in the press— given that there are two primary subjects that come to people's minds when thinking about the republic: narco-trafficking (not helped by two seasons of *Narcos* on Netflix covering both Pablo Escobar and the Cali cartel), and the "peace" with FARC—strangely not often mentioned was another of the two primary extant non-state combatants, having been around just as long as FARC, but with much less press or public attention: the Ejército de Liberación Nacional, or the ELN. This omission fascinated me for a primary reason: a distinct sense from previous experience

---

[14] I was able to see this firsthand in the Sierra Nevada de Santa Marta, in the road built between Santa Marta to Minca, Magdalena, in the mountain jungle, now touted as Colombia's "Ecological Capital"; this, and the surrounding territory, had been a FARC stronghold before being pushed out by the Colombian military and National Police.

[15] "FRONTLINE/WORLD . Colombia - The Pipeline War. Global Reach: U.S. Corporate Interests in Columbia | PBS." PBS: Public Broadcasting Service. Accessed April 8, 2019.

http://www.pbs.org/frontlineworld/stories/colombia/corporate.html.

[16] Bouvier, p.6.

and study in terms of conflict-affected countries, including research on the Cuban Revolution, that there was something important that was being distinctly overlooked. In other words, there was an important story not being told, and an important question not being asked: why has the ELN been ostensibly ignored by most contingents, despite its inherent survival for the same amount of time as FARC? Has it, as I have suspected, been underestimated?

This led me to an examination of both the history of the ELN and its current trajectory; what I have found has been alarming, at least in terms of the potential for any peace process in Colombia, but potential regional and international security issues, given Venezuela, Colombia's neighbor in South America, is also inherently in the mix on myriad levels, to be explored here later in detail in a discussion of the ELN's current status. This includes incursion in vast swaths not just of Colombia, but of Venezuela, where it has not only become deeply entrenched, but welcomed, most recently, by the Chavez and Maduro regimes. This is especially concerning should, as has been suggested by numerous sources, the United States begin once again to reinvigorate the Monroe Doctrine now in the 21st Century;[17] Venezuela has welcomed a renewed Russian and Chinese presence, given both their long-term political and resource interests, most recently bringing to Venezuela troops and financing in the first case, and arms and financing guarantees in exchange for resources in the latter.[18]

---

[17] Robbie Gramer, Keith Johnson. "Tillerson Praises Monroe Doctrine, Warns Latin America of 'Imperial? Chinese Ambitions." Foreign Policy. Last modified February 2, 2018. https://foreignpolicy.com/2018/02/02/tillerson-praises-monroe-doctrine-warns-latin-america-off-imperial-chinese-ambitions-mexico-south-america-nafta-diplomacy-trump-trade-venezuela-maduro/.

[18] Kaplan, Stephen B., and Michael Penfold. "China and Russia have deep financial ties to Venezuela. Here's what's at stake." The Washington Post. Last modified February 22, 2019.

This, along with the distinct humanitarian crisis, with over 2 million Venezuelan refugees so far having come to Colombia, with tens of thousands coming every day, taking the dangerous illicit routes across the border (incidentally, many if not most controlled by the ELN), or otherwise now being facilitated in a quasi-state capacity by ELN forces in both Colombia and Venezuela, some, including teenagers, are being lured into joining the cause for many times the monthly wage they could receive in Venezuela.[19] The reality for Colombians, Venezuelans, with incursions by the ELN into Brazil, Ecuador, Suriname, and Guyana, is both intense and distinctly overdue for examination.[20] Add to that the tensions between Venezuela and the United States, with some calling for regime change and intervention,[21] including because of the presence of illicit arms dealing, money laundering, and a distinct terrorist presence (such as Hezbollah),[22] the ELN will have an inherent, and perhaps larger role to play than anticipated, in any such consideration.

Accordingly, and in parsing this element in the mix, in this examination will be the following: a history of the ELN, including its primary influences, from its inception as a Marxist/Maoist group inspired by the Cuban Revolution, its leaders trained in Cuba by Fidel and Raul Castro and Che

https://www.washingtonpost.com/politics/2019/02/22/china-russia-have-deep-financial-ties-venezuela-heres-whats-stake/?utm_term=.8c0042e10196.

[19] This will be discussed later at length, at which point specific references will be utilized and thereby will not be utilized here.

[20] Here, I have to commend InsightCrime (http://www.insightcrime.com) for having sent up a necessary flare; they have covered this issue more than anyone, with intelligence that has been incomparable.

[21] "What a Military Intervention in Venezuela Would Look Like." Foreign Affairs. Last modified March 26, 2019. https://www.foreignaffairs.com/articles/venezuela/2019-03-19/what-military-intervention-venezuela-would-look.

[22] Clarke, Colin P. "Hezbollah Is in Venezuela to Stay." Foreign Policy. Last modified February 9, 2019. https://foreignpolicy.com/2019/02/09/hezbollah-is-in-venezuela-to-stay/.

Guevara; the combination of Marxist philosophy with liberation theology; its status as a non-state actor and combatant, including its background and strategic use of what Western military and policy describe as asymmetric/low-intensity/4GW methodology to conduct its operations; and last but not least, its current trajectory and inherent interests as not just the last remaining Colombian guerrilla group, but increasingly something much more dangerous: a force that in actuality has become, under the proverbial radar during the FARC peace process and the Venezuelan humanitarian crisis, a "Colombo-Venezuelan rebel army" that complicates not just Venezuelan-Colombian relations, but overall security across the northern half of South America.[23]

---

[23] "Op-Ed: The ELN As a Colombo-Venezuelan Rebel Army." InSight Crime. Last modified March 25, 2019. https://www.insightcrime.org/news/analysis/op-ed-the-eln-as-a-colombo-venezuelan-rebel-army/.

Part I:

Origins and Founding Philosophy

"La Violencia" and "The Agrarian Peasant"

According to U.S. military historian, Max G. Manwaring, in his examination of non-state actors in Colombia and their history, traced the impetus of the guerrilla movements to the period between the 1930's and 40's, when "chronic political, economic, and social problems created by a self-serving civilian oligarchy began to bring about yet another crisis in a long list of internal conflicts in Colombian history".[24] However, issues between two factions, Liberal and Conservative, had been in existence ostensibly since the death of Simon Bolivar; these two forces represented a "post-colonial social elite" whose power shifted between one or the other from the mid-nineteenth into the 20th Century.[25] The main issue, according to Hoskin and Maullin, was that even before the 1930's, insurgencies followed both parties, including violence as a "political action" and the end result of ideological disputes "related to Colombia's efforts to speed industrialization and to promote modern agriculture."[26] This inherently caused issues between partisans considered "peasants" (in Colombia, "peasants" are known as *Campesinos*) and "lower-class town dwellers" and those considered more elite. By 1886 a centralized system of government was imposed, and "the importance of the presidency increased," and a patronage system developed on "national, departmental, and local levels."[27] Depending upon who held the presidency, such patronage was absolute in its control of government and the spoils through to the countryside.

---

[24] Manwaring, p. 2.
[25] Hoskin, Gary, and Richard Maullin. "Soldiers, Guerrillas and Politics in Colombia." *The American Political Science Review* 71, no. 1 (1977), 389. doi:10.2307/1957041.
[26] Ibid., p. 7.
[27] Ibid., p. 8.

La Violencia--"the violence"—began in April 1948 with the murder of Liberal populist, Jorge Eliecer Gaitan, igniting the *Bogotazo*—a riot in the capital city of Bogota that caused 2,000 casualties—and prompted additional rural violence with an estimated 20,000 combatants intent on "sett[ling] old scores."[28] What was already a pronounced economic difference between the "peasant" poor and the land-holding elite in a still overwhelmingly agrarian society only became exacerbated by the political context. 129 guerrilla and bandit groups were created during *La Violencia;* 47 continued to exist in 1963, with "22 (13.8 percent) considered to be actively engaged in some form of illegal and violent activity."[29] It was also during this time that the political and economic elite pushed for even more rapid economic modernization, which as Hoskin and Maullin wryly suggest was "not necessarily of an egalitarian and democratic nature," and only heightened the "political strife," "spawned a class of men who lived by the gun," and "offered a reservoir of recruits for future political efforts requiring violence."[30]

Entering into this cacophony--the international influence of the Soviet Union, China, and Cuba post WWII--all of whom were "exporters" of political ideas, including revolution, that appealed to a certain segment of the population. Students, exposed to radical ideas in university settings, are the usual cliché; in Colombia, this was indeed a factor, but the greater context of the agrarian reality throughout Colombia, including to this day, continues to be the reason not just for the relevancy of the guerrilla groups' inceptions during this time, but for their continued existence. To understand why this is the case, immersing in that *Campesino* reality is essential.

---

[28] Manwaring, p.2.
[29] Hoskin & Maullin, p. 10.
[30] Ibid., p. 15.

Samuel Popkin, in *The Rational Peasant* (1979), delineates a reality that applies as aptly to Colombia as it did to Vietnam, about which he was writing at the time. This reality in Colombia, again, continues to exist, despite developed-world Western neo-liberal sensibilities that might be uncomfortable with such notions. As was true in the 1960's, while one might come across all of the modern conveniences in major cities; in the countryside, even today this is still *not* the case. As is also true today often in many cases between the elite and not so elite, Popkin's assertion that "within capitalist institutions...people enrich themselves only at the expense of the survival of others" and "[p]easant welfare is most precarious in precisely those areas where commercial progress is most impressive"[31] is also inherently true. Popkin, via Eric Wolf, importantly elucidates the connection between such "peasant involvement in rebellion and revolution" with "defensive reactions" and "desperate efforts to maintain subsistence arrangements that are under assault" – or find some means "to restore them once they have been lost."[32] In the best of all possible worlds, "[s]ocial norms of fairness and justice must be upheld"; "[s]ocial norms impose standards; when standards are not upheld, moral outrage and rebellion ensue."[33]

It does, but it also needs the right spark to either ignite new or resurrect old violence. And violence, in most places, is always possible, especially in rural Colombia, where economic gains of patrons or landlords, whom *Campesinos* serve for at times barely at subsistence level compensation, remain with such property holders, only aided by the continued patron system and the "growth of the

---

[31] Popkin, Samuel L. *The Rational Peasant: The Political Economy of Rural Society in Vietnam*. Oakland: University of California Press, 1979, p. 415.
[32] Ibid..
[33] Ibid., p. 420.

central state, the commercialization of agriculture, and the growth of population" who offer competition for low-wage jobs.[34] Should the "peasant class" indeed hold property, the "problem of credit and the related problem of debt bondage" can be deleterious, and "lack of land may mean not only denial of credit, but second-class citizenship as well."[35] While this should not occur in a democratic republic, it nevertheless has and does in Colombia, especially when tied to both a developing world agrarian and resource-based reality. Agrarian "peasants" represent the poorest of the poor, subsisting at the whim or mercy of a landowner, an employer, family, or, in the worst case, charity from the local church or village. This lack of stability is a matter of concern, but it is also the norm for the vast majority of rural Colombians, both then as now.

Marxism and the Cuban Revolution

From this standpoint, while democratic principles in the developed-world, "Western" view are supposed to be about Enlightenment ideals and, ostensibly, a form of humanism that can co-exist with capitalism, one can see why in the midst of such political and economic instability, with the vast history of political violence, and the threat of the divide between rich and poor becoming even more pronounced with industrialization and greater ties to the developed world (often substituting more and more for the old colonial powers[36]), the ideas of Marx (and Mao, in elevating the "peasant" class to be guerrilla heroes of revolution[37]) would appeal when seen through an idealized, philosophical lens. According to Clive Kronenberg, in

---

[34] Ibid..
[35] Ibid., p. 446.
[36] "Neocolonialism." Encyclopedia Britannica. Accessed April 9, 2019. https://www.britannica.com/topic/neocolonialism.
[37] Tse-tung, Mao. *On Guerrilla Warfare*. North Chelmsford: Courier Corporation, 2012.

writing about Marx via his influence on Che Guevara and the Cuban Revolution—which becomes relevant quickly in this examination of the ELN and its origins—the rather rapt "humanism" of Marxism, combined with the thought of revered Colombian writer and philosopher Jose Marti— espoused a "[c]ondemnation of human oppression and injustice, a core component of the humanist tradition."[38] However, this might be a bit too forgiving of Marx, whose preferences often were toward the urban proletariat rather than those of the rural persuasion early on.[39] There is also a similar urban proletariat condescension in Lenin, who believed "poor peasants would be most susceptible to propaganda and organization" when mobilization was necessary for revolution,[40] though they might not be sophisticated enough to see they were being pragmatically stereotyped and, perhaps, "herded"—like animals one is left to surmise—in service to such ideals.[41]

For Marxist ideas, or any variation thereof, to appeal to Colombian *Campesinos* and others who might be susceptible, it would indeed help tremendously to have a similar culture's influence. While university students in Colombia were all for Marxist ideology and believed in

---

[38] Kronenberg, Clive W. "Manifestations of Humanism in Revolutionary Cuba." *Latin American Perspectives* 36, no. 2 (2009), 66-80. doi:10.1177/0094582x09331953, p. 66.
[39] Vanden, Harry E. "Marxism and the Peasantry in Latin America: Marginalization or Mobilization?" *Latin American Perspectives* 9, no. 4 (1982), 74-98. doi:10.1177/0094582x8200900405, p. 74.
[40] Ibid..
[41] Here I have a distinct problem with the term "peasant" as Marx used it; as Vanden suggests, and referring, too, to the work of Edgar Nesman, there is a "general inability to understand the peasant's frame of reference"—academics and historians have been victims to a Western, urban bias; Vanden, p. 75. This is something I inherently agree with. It is one of the reasons, as I will get to later, that the developed United States, and even European allies, including those involved in any Colombian peace process, often miss the point or see insurgencies such as the ELN or FARC in such terms that lack understanding on an emotional level, even if they can on an intellectual one.

Marxist reflections on both economic equality and justice, for many in agrarian settings, it would take a Latin example to influence the proceedings and offer the greatest possible inspiration for those who were not so educated. This was only natural; rather than seeing agrarian peasants as "backward"—as did both Marx and Lenin[42]--revolutionary Cubans, even if educated, were fellow members of a once Spanish-colonized class.[43]   Additionally, according to Vanden, "[i]ndeed, one could argue that there was a tradition of peasant rebellion in Cuba long before Castro started the 26th of July movement."[44] As the same was true in Colombia, given its history, and their hero in Simon Bolivar, the issue would be the scaffold, as it were, on which to build a rebellion. Repression was a given, however, they needed an "ideological framework with which to view the struggle in larger terms".[45] Also like rural Colombia, the Sierra Maestra in Cuba "already had a well-defined tradition of peasant revolt";[46] Che Guevara and the Castros, along with their band of rag-tag revolutionaries, learned the benefit of becoming friendly, and appreciating the peasants among whom they had contact, and in many cases, needed for their survival.[47] The symbiotic relationship, as it became, was enough for Guevara to write later, "those poor, suffering,

---

[42] Vanden, p. 78.

[43] Amilcar Cabral, similarly from a former colony, also understood this reality; in Vanden (p. 80), Cabral understands the nuances of the "rural masses" enough to realize that the "peasants" can be mobilized once they gain in consciousness beyond the village, opening their eyes to see what is happening, and why the inequality is as it is, as well as who are the perpetrators of such inequality. Once they "strengthen their political awareness by assimilating the principles of national and social revolution" they "thereby become more able to play the decisive role in providing the principle force behind the liberation movement" (Vanden, p.p. 80-1.)

[44] Vanden, p. 81.
[45] Ibid..
[46] Ibid., p. 86.
[47] Ibid..

loyal inhabitants of the Sierra cannot even imagine what a great contribution they made to the forging of our revolutionary ideology."[48] Such an ideology would later prove essential for the ELN, among their *Colombiano/a* countrymen.

It is this kind of similarity, if not brotherhood between the Cuban Revolution and the eventual fostering and support of the ELN as an insurgency—along with the underlying moral component, perhaps, of Liberation Theology (see next section), that most allowed the ELN to maintain an ideological and existential resilience. Too many scholars and historians root around for an overarching theory upon which to hang their proverbial hats, when I sincerely believe that for some revolutions, such as the connected ones of Cuba and the ELN in Colombia, are because they come from a similar cultural and historic DNA. The broad spectrum of theories of revolution, and why they break out, are too vast to get into here, though many are relevant. As Jack Goldstone suggests in "Toward a Fourth Generation of Revolutionary Theory," "scholarship on the causes, processes, and outcomes of revolutions has sprawled across topics and disciplines like amoeba, stretching in various direction in response to diverse stimuli".[49] A confluence of influences here make sense, and are supported by history: on one level, Skocpol, for instance, might suggest simply that "rapid, basic transformation of a society's state and class structures...accompanied and in part carried through by class-based revolts from below"—which Goldstone suggests has been taken as the basic "standard".[50] This may indeed be relevant on a basic level, but truth is not just about the basic; it is also often about the nuances. Goldstone suggests

---

[48] Ibid..
[49] Goldstone, Jack A. "Toward a Fourth Generation of Revolutionary Theory." *SSRN Electronic Journal*, 2001. doi:10.2139/ssrn.1531902, p. 139.
[50] Ibid., p. 140.

Skocpol "ignored such matters as revolutionary ideologies, ethnic and religious bases for revolutionary mobilization, intra-elite conflicts, and the possibility of multi-class coalitions".[51]

It is, actually, perhaps simpler than that: Migdal, whom Skocpol references with dubious tone in "What Makes Peasants Revolutionary?", "argues at length that peasants in the twentieth-century Third World [what we would now call the "developing" world] face[d] an unprecedented economic crisis due to pressures from imperialism...organized revolutionary movements that offer programs to address local peasant problems is said to be one way that peasants can try to cope with the unprecedented crisis".[52] But as a side note to that, Migdal suggests that another necessary component is having been "propelled by armed revolutionary parties that have directly mobilized peasant support" in which peasant participation is "preceded by development of an organizational superstructure by students, intellectuals, and disaffected members of the middle class".[53] It would only be natural for such student-intellectual-disaffected parties to be able to put both a name on their disaffection as well as give it a target or perpetrator; this is the classic notion if this is *why* you're in a state of repression, and *who* is/are the party/parties responsible that is the foundation of any revolution when exposed, as in chemistry, to the right elements.

Seen in this light, and given the Cuban exemplar, just such Colombian university students, led by Fabio Vasquez Castano,[54] steeped in Marxism and sensitive to the socio-

---

[51] Ibid..

[52] Skocpol, Theda. "What makes peasants revolutionary?" *Social revolutions in the modern world*(n.d.), 213-239. doi:10.1017/cbo9781139173834.010, 362..

[53] Ibid..

[54] Tompkins, Jr., Paul J., and Summer Newton. "Case Studies in Insurgency and Revolutionary Warfare - Colombia (1964-2009)." United States Army

political and economic landscape, would go to Cuba to learn from the Cuban revolutionaries, and receive training for their own revolution. Again, Colombia came from a colonial past; it had a history of revolutions and political violence; it, too, was dealing with a class distinction between agrarian peasant and moneyed, land-holding elites, in which the agrarian peasants had been "a class that has been kept in ignorance" and "isolation";[55] it was being deeply affected by economic stressors of industrialization and post WWII Western imperialism: a perfect storm ripe for some kind of socio-economic-political-ideological spark to ignite a revolution. Marxism, as seen and transmitted through the Cuban lens, in which such Cubans had also taken inspiration from "historic anticolonial protagonists such as Simon Bolivar"[56] made perfect sense. Never mind two important facts: Fidel Castro himself had been in Bogota, Colombia as a student during the *Bogotazo* on April 9, 1948 and had seen the inception of *La Violencia* firsthand;[57] there was also support from Cuba to export such a revolution to Colombian soil.[58] While Castro might have argued about the specific notion of "exporting revolution," believing that "revolutions are made by the people," the significance among brothers and sisters overseas would be the "example" of the Cuban Revolution, in that "revolution is possible" and that "there are no forces capable of halting the liberation movement of the peoples".[59] However, given that those responsible for the Cuban Revolution directly trained those would lead the ELN in

---

Special Operations Command. Accessed April 9, 2019.
http://www.soc.mil/ARIS/ARIS_Colombia-BOOK.pdf, p.177.
[55] Kronenberg, p. 69.
[56] Kronenberg, p. 67.
[57] Harris, Richard L. "Cuban Internationalism, Che Guevara, and the Survival of Cuba's Socialist Regime." *Latin American Perspectives* 36, no. 3 (2009), 27-42. doi:10.1177/0094582x09334165, p. 30.
[58] Ibid., p. 31.
[59] Ibid., p. 33.

Colombia, Castro's sentiment is not wholly genuine in this case.

It is also important here to make the first true distinction between what would become ELN and FARC, including their ideological origins, as it in a sense is derived from ELN's very inception. Originating at the same time as the official military wing of the Colombian Communist Party (CCP), FARC (later, FARC-EP) was indoctrinated much more adherently to the Marxism/Leninism of the U.S.S.R and would be mostly supported by the Soviet Union. The ELN's Cuban underpinnings, in what became the ELN, were imbued with a Cuban/South American (Che, after all, was originally from Argentina[60]) Marxist/Maoist sensibilities from the beginning, including not just direct Cuban economic support, but also including proven the methods of guerrilla warfare that had been hard-won by the Cubans in the Sierra Maestra.[61]

While Che is an inordinately controversial figure, one can get insight into the Cuban revolutionary mindset via Che's often solipsistic writings, in which self-aggrandizement is ostensibly "writ large" in hindsight for posterity—however, admittedly, and deeply at times, affecting. The doctor has a choice between medical supplies and ammunition: which does he take? Is he a physician, or is he, at heart, a true guerrilla willing to die with his gun? Indeed, like any good insurgent, he chooses the ammunition.[62] Che, also having read Mao, and like Fidel and Raul Castro, acting as a commandant, learned guerrilla warfare while slogging through bodies and blood in

---

[60] Ibid., p. 29.
[61] Here it is also interesting to note that a third Colombian guerrilla group, the Ejercito de Liberacion Popular (ELP), according to Maullin (p. 16), was supplied by the third primary communist force: China.
[62] Guevara, Ernesto C. *Reminiscences of the Cuban Revolutionary War: Authorized Edition.* Sussex: Ocean Press, 2012, p. 18.

unforgiving terrain. The lessons learned about every aspect of insurgency and guerrilla warfare against a similar economic and socio-political background, including abject racism (Cubans, like Colombians, have a mixture of African, Indigenous, and Spanish blood, considered "sub-humans by imperialist machinery" with those who were "whiter" often being among the elite[63]) would be similarly pounded into those who became the ELN, reinforcing the notion of the *Campesinos* being subjugated by those most adherent to a materialist, imperialist-sympathetic and beneficiary class.

Among these lessons learned, representing the basis of guerrilla warfare, like any war, and as an interpretation, perhaps, of Clausewitz, is the choice to use violence to achieve a political aim.[64] Che "emphasized that the repressive nature of prevailing power systems made such combat 'inevitable,' 'determined by the horrifying conditions of exploitation under which the Latin American people live'";[65] and further, quoting from his hero, Jose Marti:

> Violence is not only the monopoly of the exploiters and as such the exploited can use it too and, moreover, ought to use it when the moment arrives. Marti said, "He who wages war in a country when he can avoid it is a criminal, just as he who fails to promote war which cannot be avoided is a criminal."[66]

As Kronenberg points out, here, despite Lenin's condescension toward the "agrarian peasant" the

---

[63] Kronenberg, p. 70.
[64] Daase, Christopher. "Clausewitz and Small Wars." *Clausewitz in the Twenty-First Century*, 2007, 182-195. doi:10.1093/acprof:oso/9780199232024.003.0011, p. 10.
[65] Kronenberg, p. 69.
[66] Ibid..

overarching understanding that "as long as there is exploitation of man by man, wars are inevitable."[67]

Taking this as justification for violence, revolution necessitates training to harness such violence, when necessary toward such a political end. As Stathis Kalyvas suggests in *The Logic of Violence in Civil War* (2006), there is a need to "decouple" the notion of civil war itself as "conflict" from the inherent "violence" in civil war.[68] Revolution, carried out by an organized force, resorting to armed violence over a specific period of time, and toward a specific political end, is the very definition of civil war. However, as Kalyvas points out, civil war is a state that carries with it a certain kind of legitimacy; violence is a tactic.[69] War, despite deviating political leanings, is nevertheless given tendency toward certain monolithic truths; Che and Clauzewitz may as well have been on the same page in terms of this distinction: no matter the similarities in terms of civil war itself, each case in which such violence is necessary is going to be inherently unique.[70] And, to bring home the point of their synergy, according to Che, the violence in civil war will always be a response because no matter what, "the general methods of oppression are always the same."[71] Violence for the sake of violence—without it being a specific tactic utilized in specific instances toward the process of a political objective—can be a "homicidal impulse", and while this may be evident in any insurgency, there is a big difference between this "dysfunctional violence" (microcosm) and the "systemic functional violence" of conflict in civil war (macrocosm).[72]

---

[67] Ibid., p. 70.
[68] Kalyvas, Stathis N. *The Logic of Violence in Civil War*. Cambridge: Cambridge University Press, 2006, p. 5.
[69] Ibid., p. 16
[70] Ibid., p. 7.
[71] Ibid., p. 9.
[72] Ibid., p. 19.

And there is a reason this is important: the kind of insurgency and civil war fought by the Cubans in the revolution and taught to what would become the ELN in Colombia was dependent upon the very people among whom the insurgents were fighting, and in a remote terrain in the "countryside" where they would be "supported by the long oppressed rural masses."[73] This is one of the fundamental pillars, as it were, of the kind of Maoist/Cuban guerrilla war strategy that was lost on the state, and at times, and in time, on the guerrilla forces themselves given enough longevity. These agrarian masses, in Che's inimitable insurgent mentality, were essential to "provide material support and recruits for the guerrilla groups which through armed struggle would smash the forces that had long suppressed them. For their support the guerrillas would become their saviors".[74] Indeed, this was the thought. As was the notion that the "peasants, then are expected to immediately see the virtue of the guerrilla struggle"[75] which was not true in all cases where the people could not be swayed by the benefits of the *guerra de guerrilla*. This was proved to those who would become the ELN by the Cuban example; the leadership of the insurgency needed to be in tune with the people among whom they were residing—enough to become one of them—not just offering protection and fighting for a purported, if beneficial common cause, but able to prove the benefit of such an insurgency and be drawn into it by the promise of its aims. Only then would the revolutionary leadership, "with an organizational framework capable of absorbing peasants and then expanding power through their recruitment" be sustained.[76] This was also a hard lesson won

---

[73] Vanden, p. 86.
[74] Ibid..
[75] Ibid., p. 87.
[76] Skocpol, p. 364.

in the Sierra Maestra, as Che himself expounds upon in *Guerrilla Warfare* (1961):

> It is important to emphasize that guerrilla warfare is a war of the masses, a war of the people. The guerrilla band is an armed nucleus, the fighting vanguard of the people. It draws great force from the mass of the people themselves... The guerrilla fighter needs full help from the people of the area. This is an indispensable condition. This is clearly seen by considering the bandit gangs that operate in a region... The only thing missing is support of the people; and inevitably, these gangs are captured and exterminated by public force... [T]he guerrilla fighter is a social reformer, that he takes up arms responding to the angry protest of the people against their oppressors, and that he fights in order to change the social system that keeps all of his unarmed brothers in ignominy and misery.[77]

To then maintain legitimacy among the people, one must be ostensibly fighting for them, and any "dysfunctional violence" would be counter to that cause; only that which must be leveled, either in defense of the people, or to maintain the objective via legitimate means in terms of spies, traitors, or even guerrilla themselves who go against this philosophy, can be tolerated.

In not getting into the vast specifics of the guerrilla strategy and tactics here, as it would require a book unto itself, and this has already been done by both Mao and Guevara, whose understandings are inordinately similar—it is enough to perhaps point out that Che utilized Mao in his own thinking and applied those lessons to his own

---

[77] Guevara, Ernesto. *Che Guevara on Guerrilla Warfare*. New York: Praeger, 1961, p.p. 4-5.

experience.[78] Certain nuances, though, are important, so they will be covered here. But first, it's necessary to offer a contextual, societal framework via Kalyvas, who takes a macro-to-micro view of civil war and breaks down such conflict into three tiers that are essential in understanding the relationships among those involved. This, upon reflection, seems inherently logical, but in parsing the strategy of the insurgency as conducted by the Cubans and taught to what would become the ELN, it needs, perhaps to be reiterated.

For Kalyvas, the three structural components of societal engagement that are relevant, are:

1) the "elites" who are indeed "political actors" and among whom they may be represented by either/both state- and non-state parties or individuals;

2) the "meso" tier, in which the "elites" interact with the populations over whom they either rule or exist; and

3) "intimate" parties, in which there is "interaction within small groups and among individuals".[79]

For both Mao and Guevara, it is in this third tier that an insurgency/guerrilla force finds its strength. It is here that both the benefits and the challenges of guerrilla warfare are at their most profound. It is this inherent intimacy of conflict—and violence—within their midst that reinforces the stakes, and where a guerrilla force can tell whether or not

---

[78] In terms of strategy and tactics themselves, these are the subjects of entire books, so I will not get into them here in detail. But the "playbooks" can be represented by the two books on guerrilla warfare by both Mao and Che, both titled *Guerrilla Warfare*, which are worth reading in their entirety, and which I used as a foundation of understanding both the Cuban Revolution and its impact on the ELN. I will, however, give a basic understanding of certain tenets here, which will be referenced further in a later section from the Western/developed world perspective, which will be relevant in terms of the ELN's current status.

[79] Kalyvas, p. 9.

their strategy—and tactics—are working on the level at which they command their most direct support.[80] It is also where the root ideology is spread to not just bolster the pragmatic foundation to the insurgency, but a philosophical one as well, and among intimates.[81] For both the Cuban Revolution and what would become the ELN's own insurgency via guerilla warfare, what Skocpol would suggest, rather intellectually via Eric Wolf, are "parochial reactions to major social dislocations, set in motion by overwhelming societal change" can indeed be put more simply, as Che/Castros did, and as would the ELN, as the reaction of the peasant classes to *"imperial Western capitalism"* [emphasis: Skocpol] as manifested, accepted, and promulgated by the elite class to the detriment of their own countrymen and women. The notion that "intrusive capitalism [had] upset the prior balances" and had created increasingly more intensive "exploitative relationships" between elites and the lower classes,[82] could be proven at the intimate, third tier, subsistence level of rural communities. That the supreme overlord, as it were, from which the elites were deriving rather addictive spoils, would be the imperialistic Western powers, only gave these communities a large, evocative target that existed, ominously, somewhere out there—but which had a direct effect on their own lives, and from which the elite classes inherently benefitted. They did not need to be reminded of the dire nature of their security; this was obvious. But the insurgents could, again, point to those who were responsible, and this was the pragmatic, logical, and yet profoundly emotional hook needed to enlist their support.

---

[80] Skocpol, p. 365.

[81] This is the original "hearts and minds" philosophy made so famous by Western war methodology in bringing to a guerrilla war zone a counter-insurgency (COIN).

[82] Skocpol, p. 368.

Once this kind of understanding was achieved through convincing such communities of their role in their common interests—and stakes—via what most would consider an inherent propaganda, it would, however, only be through action that any such community would give full support, for as Vanden points out, the "peasants, then, are expected to immediately see the virtue of the guerrilla struggle" for "the most important form of propaganda is successful military action."[83] It is here that what was learned by the students in Cuba, who would become the ELN, and led by Fabio Vasquez, adopted both the foundation of guerrilla theory and the specific strategies and tactics through which to exercise it. However, the foundational "truths" that were first necessary to internalize were, as championed by the Castros, and especially Guevara, were:

1) Popular forces can win a war against the army [state forces];
2) It is not necessary to wait until all conditions for making revolution exist; the insurrection can create them;
3) In underdeveloped America the countryside is the basic area for armed fighting.[84]

From here, once these truths are internalized, the strategy and tactics will make sense; this includes the normal array of guerrilla warfare strategies and respective tactics that have become almost rote among those familiar with any military history involving asymmetric warfare: use of local resources; inherent mobility and flexibility; popular support for food, medical supplies, etc., if they can't be procured otherwise; pragmatic use of all material and munitions as one won't always know when there will be re-supply; attacking and harassing the enemy where it least expects it;

---

[83] Vanden, p. 87.
[84] Guevara (Guerrilla Warfare), p. 2.

the psychological weapon of creating the sense that the enemy is "surrounded" and does not know who in the community is friendly or an insurgent; munitions should be utilized both offensively and defensively, but the goal is to target what is most symbolic of state strength; inherent unpredictability in not knowing when the insurgency will strike; and using the sheer size of any state force, including any tendency toward bureaucratized action, against it.[85] But most important: the solidarity, loyalty, and support of the people among—and for whom—the insurgency is fighting. To gain the initiative, one cannot solely know what should be done both strategically and tactically, *you have to know that the community is behind you* [my emphasis]. While this may be true for state forces as well in a more macro sense, it is never more important than in the micro sense in an intimate setting, and among those who are supposed to be the very reason for the revolution and its respective guerrilla insurgency.

For what would become the ELN, the specific military theory adopted at the time was that used by the Cubans, *foquismo*, or in English, "foco theory".[86] The foco model was ostensibly that suggested above, but the emphasis was on "small, focused groups of guerrillas" that "conducted small, strategic attacks" while they "dispersed dissent throughout the countryside".[87] This also "emphasized targeting specific areas of the government infrastructure, with the goal of destabilization"[88]. It was with this that the ELN "began its revolution in earnest" when it got back to Colombia, where it "dispersed throughout Colombia" in "at least twenty-three Colombian departments and an area from

---

[85] Thornton, Rod. *Asymmetric Warfare: Threat and Response in the 21st Century*. Cambridge: Polity, 2007.

[86] Tompkins & Newman, p. 177.

[87] Ibid., p. 178.

[88] Ibid..

Narino in the extreme south, La Guajira in the north, Aurca in the east, and Choco on the Pacific coast."[89] These "nuclei" represented guerrilla *frentes,* or (in English) fronts.[90] As Tompkins and Newton note, the "wide dispersal complicate[d] verification and force protection"[91]—when the ELN struck, the capacity to retreat back and remain undiscovered, as is optimal in guerrilla operations, was essential. The "incubation" of the ELN's foco structure centered out of the rural San Vincente de Chucuri in the department of Santander; it had "rugged geography that allowed clandestine mobilization," "traditions of rebellion, peasant struggles, and a familiarity with violence and dissent" along with "several villages with peasants with former guerrilla experience" that would have an "ideological affinity".[92] Vasquez "ingratiated himself among into the community" for a period of time; working alongside *Campesinos,* he was able to both speak the language of both local history and dissent they understood, while referencing common figures known to all, among them Jose Antonio Galan, "the first peasant to rebel against the Spanish" who had been "hanged for insurrection" and was, conveniently enough, from Santander.[93]

In due course, Vasquez was able to set up a jungle camp and begin training a cadre of "a few dozen villagers" for their first operation. This would be in Simacota on January 7, 1965, in which "fewer that thirty guerrillas opened fire, kill[ed] two policemen, and distributed their manifesto".[94] The operation gained "much publicity" and was considered a success.[95]

---

[89] Ibid..
[90] Ibid..
[91] Ibid., p. 179.
[92] Ibid..
[93] Ibid., p. 180.
[94] Ibid..
[95] Ibid..

The Introduction and Incorporation of Liberation Theology

Whereas the ELN at this point had the initiative, as well as both the general ideological and pragmatic foundations of insurgency as ingrained from their Cuban training and promulgation of Marxism, where the ELN would also differ significantly from FARC or any of the other armed, non-state combatants (whether eventually EPL, M-19, right-wing paramilitaries under the AUC umbrella, or narco-syndicates[96]), would be the addition of a unique, but powerful element into their ideological framework: the introduction of Liberation Theology as a spiritual component of what would otherwise have been solely a Marxist/Maoist-based revolution. For some, this might seem a contradiction in terms; Marxism is known for its secular nature, even if it can incorporate, as Kronenberg would suggest, a distinctly humanist tone. However, given the religious nature of most Colombians, in which Catholicism is endemic among the population, and especially in rural areas, where the Catholic Church holds sway in many matters and can be a focal point in a dispersed agrarian area, its inclusion into the overall ideology of the ELN was one of the reasons for its resilience—and, perhaps, its continued existence.

It is one thing to have the political interests of a community behind an insurgency, including supply, support, and even individuals willing to be combatants; but as Davies suggests, once one goes beyond basic physical needs (here he delineates "food, clothing, shelter, [physical] health, and safety from bodily harm"[97]), as important are social ties— "affectional" of "family and friends"—as well as some

---

[96] These will be discussed later.
[97] Davies, James C. "Toward a Theory of Revolution." *American Sociological Review* 27, no. 1 (1962), 5. doi:10.2307/2089714, p. 8.

semblance of "equal dignity and justice".[98] To have a "revolutionary state of mind," one needs to also have the "necessary additional ingredient [of] a persistent, unrelenting threat...which puts them in the mental state where they believe they will not be able to satisfy one or more basic needs."[99] The threat, already identified, of the elites feeding at the trough proffered by the greedy imperialist, developed world while the rural communities suffered, is already a powerful political and economic inducement to either engage in, or support, a revolutionary cadre of countrymen who seem to speak for the people and liberate them. But add to that something else which not only fundamentally solidifies insurrectionary justification for insurgency politically, but also speaks to the notions of equal dignity and justice with priests representing a moral authority as combatants, giving insurgents ostensibly a spiritually-sanctioned reason for revolution. To those who are more secular in nature, this may not seem important; to those for whom religion is what they turn to in times of pain, hardship, or oppression as the one thing that offers solace, it is a key unlocking a divinely-prescribed permission to wage war for the protection of the community.

The ELN, following its first success in Simacota, attracted just such an influence in priests inspired by Vatican II and subsequent shifts within the Catholic Church who brought a more radicalized form of Catholic thought to the revolution.[100] It was one that suggested not only that the Catholic Church up to that point had failed its congregations, but that people didn't need to wait for "some misty paradise beyond the pale distant clouds" and instead should "create a just society on Earth"—a "Kingdom of God" that existed

---

[98] Ibid..
[99] Ibid..
[100] Ibid..

"here and now".[101] As part of the radicalization of certain institutions in the 1960's and 1970's, this new Catholic movement also opposed "trenchant conservative politics" while supporting "transformation and distributive social justice" that might "eradicate dependency, poverty, and injustice"; this contradicted the previous tendency of the Church to solely "legitimate and reproduce the power and authority of the capitalist state" that was so endemic to both elites and Western imperialism.[102] Marx himself had "understood the extortionate and unscrupulous characteristics of Christianity and how it was turned into a profiteering caricature of the Gospels"—especially when "Christianity became the God of empire".[103] Those who fully advocated this new thinking also brought along the notion that there was a difference between "living labor"— that which encompassed the idea of the possibility of liberation on an individual and community level, and the "objectified labor" that served as "the means and instruments of production" that had "no role in the liberation from oppression".[104] "Social change" came from "collective action"—but for right and common purpose, rather than facilitating "structures of privilege [that] will never willingly abdicate what they consider to be their birthright".[105] Referencing Collier, McLaren relates liberation theological premises to the notion that "[s]o long as human authority exists, it should as far as possible be organized so that the greatest power serves the least powerful with all its might".[106] This was concurrent with a growing sentiment in

[101] McLaren, Peter, and Petar Jandrić. "Karl Marx and Liberation Theology: Dialectical Materialism and Christian Spirituality in, against, and beyond Contemporary Capitalism." *tripleC: Communication, Capitalism & Critique. Open Access Journal for a Global Sustainable Information Society* 16, no. 2 (2018), 598-607. doi:10.31269/triplec.v16i2.965, p. 599.
[102] Ibid..
[103] Ibid..
[104] Ibid., p.p. 599-600.
[105] Ibid., p. 602.
[106] Ibid..

Latin America that even the Church was too dependent upon the elite; "changes in the Catholic Church [were] either instigated by elites or only [became] widely disseminated" with "elite approval," and "[d]ue to the hierarchical control of the Catholic Church, innovations and movements they inspire falter when the elites withdraw their support".[107]

The combination of such thought, by virtue of the vanguard in the ELN of these priests, among them, Colombian Camino Torres, who proved himself worthy to join following seven months' observation, followed by guerrilla training to be indoctrinated into the insurgency as, ostensibly, the ELN's version of a warrior-priest.[108] Despite Torres not having survived his first engagement in 1966, he was followed by other priests, including from Spain, among them Manuel Perez, *nom de guerre* "El Cura,"[109] who would continue the hybrid Marxist/Liberation Theological mission and spread it among both combatants and community. With the influence of such presences, it seemed, again, that there was a necessary, reinforcing symbiosis of both the temporal and theological that appealed to those among whom the ELN would draw their support. In fact, the liberation theological emphasis seemed to be the vanguard, as in 1968, a Conference of Catholic bishops in Latin America convened in Medellin, Colombia, stating that the Church had been in "structural sin" and that the Church needed to now focus its solidarity not on the guidance and preferences of the elites in the Church, but on the needs of the poor.[110] This included challenging "oppressive state regimes, calling for respect for human rights and democratization" among the laity.[111] From

---

[107] Mackin, Robert S. "Liberation Theology: The Radicalization of Social Catholic Movements." *Politics, Religion & Ideology* 13, no. 3 (2012), 333-351. doi:10.1080/21567689.2012.698979, p. 335.
[108] Tompkins & Newton, p. 180.
[109] Ibid..
[110] Mackin., p. 333.
[111] Ibid., p. 336..

this came the denouncing of *desarrollismo*—"developmentalism"—in which foreign investment with the "injection" of foreign, developed-world capital, along with the "massive exploitation of Amazonia…was sustained by the ideology of progress".[112] This "indictment of developmentalism" that only benefitted the elites, but "contributed to increased social inequality" seemed to smack of a new form of colonialism, based on developed-world belief that anyone not white and Christian was "subhuman".[113] In this sense, "[m]odernity, capitalism and coloniality" could only be interpreted as "closely-linked phenomena".[114]

Coming from such a powerfully combined foundation of political, socio-economic, and theological belief, the ELN would buck against this "coloniality of power"[115] not just in terms of the outside developed world, but the elite structures within Colombia itself, and it would soon find itself up against not just the Colombian state, but FARC (which was created two years after the ELN from the CCP) and other insurgent groups, *narcos*, and the tacitly state-sanctioned paramilitaries, who as Manwaring suggests in their totality, to this day, not only would "threaten Colombia's survival as an organized democratic state," but it would also "undermine the stability and sovereignty of its neighbors".[116]

Such a warning would seem, today, appropriately prophetic.

---

[112] Mackin, Robert S. "Liberation Theology: The Radicalization of Social Catholic Movements." *Politics, Religion & Ideology* 13, no. 3 (2012), 333-351. doi:10.1080/21567689.2012.698979, p.p. 621-2.
[113] Ibid., p.p. 622-3.
[114] Ibid., p. 624.
[115] Ibid., p. 626.
[116] Manwaring, p. 3.

PART II: North vs. South:

The United States, Colombia, and the ELN to 2017

Introduction

It is here, now that the philosophical and historical context has been established, that it's important to bring in an additional factor not only in terms of the success—and failure—of Colombia's response to the ELN from myriad perspectives, but the implications, until 2018—when there was a pronounced shift in the proceedings with the election of Ivan Duque to the Colombian presidency—for Colombia, South America, and indeed, the Western Hemisphere. While the EU (inclusive of involvement individually of various member states) has had an impact on Colombia and its peace and development processes via "soft" power, for better or worse, the United States has had a far more significant—and active—role in Colombia's responses to non-state actors. For this reason, when it comes to defining the ELN's role and trajectory in a larger context, the United States, given its interests in Colombia, the aid—monetary, tactical, and military—it has given, inclusive of Plan Colombia and/or associated Stability and Support Operations (SASO), and including any national interests or any perceived threats— has had, for better or worse, the role of a stakeholder. Because of this, and because of its military involvement in training the Colombian military (including its *Policia Nacional*), this has had a direct effect on Colombian military strategies and tactics among non-state combatants.

This is why I am going to switch tacks here; before getting into the ELN during this time period, one needs to have a sense of context of the United States in involving itself in Colombia and the perspective that has impacted U.S.-Colombian relations. Many forget the U.S. was both an overt and covert stakeholder and influence in Colombia even before the ubiquity of the U.S.'s failing "War on Drugs." No other foreign country has spent more on the Colombian state than the United States; in the last decades, this had been in terms of Plan Colombia; there is also a current defense partnership in terms of the US (via SOCOM) and Colombian armed forces.[117] Interventions by the U.S., which have been perceived to be in U.S. national interest in terms of security (of both the homeland against narco-trafficking and in support of the security of U.S.-based conglomerates), have included money, weapons, technology, and tactical advisors from both military and law enforcement. Because of this influence, it is necessary to examine the underlying theories of how to go about countering such illicit groups, including as during the 1970's and 80's through to the present, when a critical axis of armed violence, insurgency, and narco-criminality caused Western developed powers to engage what otherwise would have been a solely Colombian civil war.

Small Wars, Fourth Generation Warfare, Asymmetry, Stability and Support Operations (SASO), and Counterinsurgency (COIN)

The first element to address, for such context, is the Western, developed-world theory of war itself. If one is going to combat an insurgency, it helps to know how best to approach it, and from what foundational perspective. Here, the first element is always the political notion of the state, and how to protect the state from attack, from either within or without. The fallback in Western (and developed world) theories of modern war comes from this starting point of the state; here there is usually not one theorist who will neglect to mention Westphalian notions of the state as derived from the Treaty of Westphalia in 1640, ending the Thirty Years' War.[118] From the many different contingents who might

---

[117] "Colombian President-elect Ivan Duque Visits U.S. Southern Command." U.S. Southern Command. Last modified July 14, 2018. https://www.southcom.mil/MEDIA/NEWS-ARTICLES/Article/1575023/colombian-president-elect-ivan-duque-visits-us-southern-command/.

[118] Lind, William S. "Understanding Fourth Generation War." *Military Review*, September/October 2004, 12-16, p. 12.

wage war against one another, this ostensibly, according to many scholars, established the notion that nation-states[119] would wage war as such, and with a specific state military apparatus to do so.[120]

Attention to Clausewitz invariably comes next. Carl von Clausewitz, a German general, wrote what is considered the seminal Western tract on what was then modern warfare, titled *On War* (1832).[121] *On War* is required reading at most Western war colleges and university courses on modern war, but as Christopher Daase wryly suggests, what is also important to know is that "Clausewitz is more often cited than read."[122] There have been many who have purported to understand the nuances of Clausewitz, including where he offered commentary on what is today considered "small wars," but much of it, as both Daase and Waldman contend, has been cherry-picked, vitiated, and quoted out of context.[123] Clausewitz is more complex and nuanced than many understand him to be, whether military or policy advisors realize it or not; instead, many see him as only advocating a kind of machine like war strategy—the ultimate in what would come to be seen as Western rationalism through a militaristic lens.[124] This pre-supposes that policy

[119] "Nation State: A Glossary of Political Economy Terms - Dr. Paul M. Johnson." Auburn University. Accessed April 10, 2019.
http://www.auburn.edu/~johnspm/gloss/nation_state.: "A form of state in which those who exercise power claim legitimacy for their rule partly or solely on the grounds that their power is exercised for the promotion of the distinctive interests, values and cultural heritage of a particular nation whose members ideally would constitute all, or most of, its subject population and all of whom would dwell within the borders."
[120] Lind., p. 12.
[121] Clausewitz, Carl V. *On War*. 1832.
[122] Daase, Christopher. "Clausewitz and Small Wars." *Clausewitz in the Twenty-First Century*, 2007, 182-195.
doi:10.1093/acprof:oso/9780199232024.003.0011, p. 2.
[123] Waldman, Thomas. "Politics and War: Clausewitz's Paradoxical Equation." *Parameters*, Fall 2010, 1-13.
https://www.clausewitz.com/opencourseware/Waldman2.pdf, p. 2.
[124] Ibid., p. 3.

can be suitably and mechanistically operationalized in terms of doctrine, down to strategy, and then to tactics—though even Clausewitz knew, all too well, that no war was so neat and tidy; war, involving human beings and all of their complexities, meant "that any strictly logical solution is impossible".[125] Waldman, in quoting Echervarria, points out what to most should be obvious: "War involves living forces rather than static elements; thus, it can change quickly and significantly in ways the logic of policy may not expect."[126]

However, those in the Western military who prefer the more machine-like metaphor and associate this with a Clausewitz "doctrine" on the conduct of war miss his point regarding belligerents, and even guerrilla forces, whom Clausewitz specifically referenced when speaking about Tyrolean uprising, and the Spanish insurrection starting in 1809.[127] Regarding these, even before Mao, as "people's wars," he delineated what today would be a salient definition of "small wars" which, in today's language, is an "application of organized and unorganized violence by non-state actors against military forces to harass and exhaust the enemy's army in order to change his policy."[128] Here one can then differentiate "big wars" (between states) from "small wars" (states against non-state actors).[129]

But to some, such as Mary Kaldor who suggests Clausewitz is representative of "old wars," or David Keen, who transposes the usual "Clausewitzian" phrasing to suggest that war is "no longer politics, but economics by other means,"[130] Clausewitz, despite his suggestion that "belligerents in war generally act according to their

---

[125] Ibid., p. 4.
[126] Ibid., p. 5.
[127] Daase, p. 2.
[128] Ibid., p. 4.
[129] Ibid., p. 5.
[130] Ibid., p. 2.

objectives, they do so in a complex, multilateral, and interactive environment pervaded by uncontrollable external political dynamics and chance occurrences"—is somehow no longer relevant.[131] This is because "new" wisdom will invariably supplant the "old" and new theories and doctrines will be espoused if only to try to make war more comprehensible in the language of the modern world, even if the old wisdom still applies.

But some delineations can be helpful, especially if grounded in history and a change in thinking from certain generations to the next in a progression that can be effectively tracked. In reflecting upon the proxy wars of the Cold War in which the U.S. was embroiled with boots on the ground, such as Korea and Vietnam, in the 1980's, William S. Lind, in working with the U.S. Marine Corps, proposed a means of studying war via four generations of modern war.[132] These are: 1) "massed manpower" via "line-and-column" tactics, 2) "attrition" via "firepower" in which "the artillery conquers, the infantry occupies," 3) maneuvering capacity via "speed, surprise, and mental as well as physical dislocation" in which non-linear fighting (not front to front) means collapsing the enemy from "the rear forward,"[133] 4) non-state war "that employs all available networks—political, economic, social, military—to convince an opponent…that their strategic goals are either unachievable or too costly".[134]

Fourth Generation warfare (4GW or Gen4) has "become popular" as a subject, according to Echevarria, because of "recent twists"—the wars in Iraq and

---

[131] Waldman, p. 6.
[132] Lind, William S. "Understanding Fourth Generation War." *Military Review*, September/October 2004, 12-16.
[133] Lind, p.p. 12-13.
[134] Echevarria II, Antulio J. "Fourth-Generation War and Other Myths." *Strategic Studies Institute*, November 2008, i. - 21. https://ssi.armywarcollege.edu/pdffiles/PUB632.pdf, p. v.

Afghanistan[135]--considered "non-trinitarian".[136] Lind suggests that the U.S. military, for the most part, is not prepared to fight a Gen4 war on its own terms, using instead Gen2 or Gen3 warfare or some combination thereof; Gen4 combatants "will not sign up to the Geneva conventions, but some might still be open to a chivalric code governing how war with them would be fought."[137] (Incidentally, the ELN has just such official codes of conduct.[138]) The issue: this is seen, from the U.S./Western perspective as an inherently asymmetric conflict. This asymmetry is defined by Rod Thornton as "the weak against the strong," or "the West being challenged in a *new* way by significantly smaller and less powerful entities" who are "weak adversaries who make up for such weakness in their skill, dexterity, nimbleness, intelligence, and above all, in their zeal, their will to win".[139] According to Kenneth McKenzie, Jr., this includes the notion that:

> Our ability to even entertain the possibility of intervention is linked to our vast superiority in mobility (both strategic and tactical), command and control, and advanced weapons. Applied intelligently…there are identifiable, addressable pressure points in virtually any society—or sub-society—which we can reach and target. If these entities are waging fourth generation warfare, it will

---

[135] Ibid., p. i.

[136] "Trinitarian war," hearkening back to a misreading of Clausewitz: 1) the people, 2) the military, and 3) the state. This, rather than the actual Clausewitz "trinity" which is, 1) "basic hostility, which if unchecked would make war spiral out of control," 2) "chance and uncertainty, which defy prescriptive doctrines and make war unpredictable," and 3) "the attempt to use war to achieve a purpose, and direct it toward an end." One can see here that the second trinity provides the "what" to the first trinity's "who."

[137] Lind., p. 14.

[138] International Committee of the Red Cross. Accessed May 8, 2019. https://www.icrc.org/en/download/file/13953/irrc-882-codes-conduct.pdf.

[139] Thornton, Rod. *Asymmetric Warfare: Threat and Response in the 21st Century*. Cambridge: Polity, 2007, p.p. vii-viii.

not require a fourth generation response by the West to intervene…if targeted against the proper centers of gravity and employed as part of a larger application of all of the elements of our power: military, economic, and diplomatic.[140]

Lind would disagree with this assessment, writing that this is actually a situation in which the state loses its power: "we are the weaker, not the stronger party, despite all of our firepower and technology".[141] There are different reasons for this, according to Lind; one is that unless one is part of Special Operations Forces (SOF), integration of troops with the local people goes against force protection, which would "hurt us badly"; another issue is a definition of "wins"—the U.S. military determines "in terms of comparative attrition rates" and not enough at "operational, strategic, mental, and moral levels".[142] One has to take the view of the Gen4 forces, in that at times, you have to "lose to win".[143] This includes, importantly, when you're operating on a community level where "cultural intelligence is vital"; this means not spiking the proverbial football— "humiliating the defeated enemy troops, especially in front of their own population" which is "always a serious mistake but one that Americans are prone to make."[144] (Note: even Clausewitz suggested this: if one tries to "demoralize" rebels by "demonizing" them or applying "inhumane treatment or executions," it will ramp up the violence as the insurgents must "repay atrocity with atrocity, violence with violence."[145])

---

[140] McKenzie, Jr., Kenneth F. "Elegant irrelevance: fourth-generation warfare." *Parameters*, Fall 1993, 51-60, p. 58.
[141] Lind., p. 15.
[142] Ibid..
[143] Ibid..
[144] Ibid..
[145] Daase, p. 6.

But most importantly, Western forces need to address that it is going up against a guerrilla, insurgent mindset[146]--or in other words, realizing that these kinds of wars operate on a much more personal playing field—the "intimate" tier that Kalyvas described when it came to civil wars and violence. According to Lind, because we're not fighting state-to-state wars for the most part (including nuclear war) and are instead more and more dealing with proxy conflicts or asymmetric conflicts with non-state actors, we are heading toward a greater prevalence of wars that "return to the way war worked before the rise of the state...[n]ow, as then, many different entities, not just governments of states, will wage war, and they will wage war for many different reasons, not just 'the extension of politics by other means".[147] This also goes back to Daase in his discussion of small wars: the notions of victory are different between combatants in an asymmetric setting, even if it includes the idea that one can "lose small wars strategically and yet be successful politically"—and that the paradigm is often switched: the "weaker" insurgent force acts "tactically in the offensive and strategically in the defensive" in "struggles for political legitimacy and recognition."[148] The reason this is important: once again, in going back to the guerrilla handbook, as it were, it's about the people—the communities—because this is the site of the most strength—and vulnerability.

For this reason, there is something to be inherently learned from the Gen4 perspective, even if its legitimacy continues to be questioned. Many in the West still cannot fathom the idea of even examining war (again, aside from SOF) from this or a similar paradigm despite having seen it among combatants most recently in Vietnam, Iraq, and

---

[146] Lind, p. 15.
[147] Ibid..
[148] Daase, p. 6.

Afghanistan, MENA, among many other asymmetric wars with guerrillas/insurgencies. The mentality is still predominantly imbued with McKenzie's hubris at both a strategic and an operational level: that of inherent and unquestioned countering superiority via sheer numbers, strategy, firepower, and technology. The West, including the United States, lends its support, or engages via stability and support operations (SASO) and counter-insurgency operations (COIN), "and related mission sets",[149] so how it operates, and from what mindset is essential in understanding its part in the mix of Colombia's past, its current course, and its future trajectory—along with those forces it has been and will be up against.

Although I have been using "guerrilla group" and "insurgency" somewhat interchangeably so far, for the purposes of SASO and COIN, it would be good to define "insurgent" given the Western/developed-world context; according to Paul Stanisland in *Networks of Rebellion* (2014), an insurgent group is one that "claim[s] to be a collective organization that has a name to designate itself, is made of formal structures of command and control, and intends to seize political power using violence."[150] Further: "[i]nsurgent groups have central processes of decision-making and institution-building and local processes of recruitment and tactical control".[151] He then differentiates further central from local control:

- "Robust central control...coordinates its strategy and retains its leaders' loyalty and unity as it implements strategy"; "it establishes and maintains institutions for monitory cadres, creating ideological 'party lines' that socialize

---

[149] Bunker, Robert. *Old and New Insurgency Forms*. Perennial Press, 2018, p.1.
[150] Staniland, Paul. *Networks of Rebellion: Explaining Insurgent Cohesion and Collapse*. Ithaca: Cornell University Press, 2014, p. 5.
[151] Ibid..

new members, engage in diplomacy, and
distribute resources";

- "Strong local control...processes involve
reliably consistent obedience from foot soldiers
and low-ranking commanders"; institutions exist
on the ground to recruit and socialize fighters
who become loyal to the leadership".[152]

He continues: "The initial organization of an insurgent group
reflects the networks and institutions in which its leaders
were embedded prior to violent mobilization" which then
"act as politicized opposition to state power."[153] And here,
he mentions the guerrilla connection: "[r]oughly half of post-
1945 civil wars have been waged as irregular guerrilla
groups."[154]

The bottom line of the struggle between insurgency
and COIN, he says, is ultimately about "who can access and
control society" given that both state capacities and the
makeup and capacity of guerrilla groups are different from
one situation to the next and logically "present different
challenges".[155] But the key of any COIN effort is
"understanding why organizations fail and collapse is just as
important as explaining how they adapt and innovate".[156]
There are two "mechanisms" that "drive change"[157]:

- "Comprehensive counterinsurgency" which
targets leaders and in which the state maintains
and regains control of locals; and

---

[152] Ibid..
[153] Ibid., p. 9.
[154] Ibid., p. 10.
[155] Ibid., p. 36.
[156] Ibid., p. 38.
[157] Ibid..

- "Mismanaged   expansion   by   insurgent leaders".[158]

Countering the COIN efforts—like COIN efforts themselves—involve insurgents' capacity to "erode the opponent's will to fight rather than destroying his means"[159]; it also deals with each trying to make the other into the boogey man, as it were—and in the case of the U.S., some elite, monolithic, imperialist, evil force[160] while any insurgency is going to be seen as cruel, bloody, violent (using "illegitimate" violence), and using indiscriminate terrorist tactics, if not being delegitimized as a recognized army and deemed, officially by the state, "terrorists" instead.[161] In both cases, as Greg Simons writes, whatever "clash" is ultimately going to come down to the strength of two factors: perception and commitment.[162] Neither insurgency nor COIN can transcend these in terms of importance, and either can determine the extent to which either will "fail and collapse" or "adapt and innovate" whether on a micro or macro level.

But these are, as are all aspects in this section, general tenets; again, these are steeped in theory and generalizations that may seem logical, but again, the rub is to operationalize them, so the specifics of each situation and engagement are important, as are the nuances. Every theorist who has ever been in the trenches knows that there is a big difference between coming up with strategy and tactics and

---

[158] Ibid., p. 39.
[159] Echevarria, p. 10.
[160] "Former Undercover CIA Officer Talks War And Peace." *YouTube*. June 13, 2016. https://www.youtube.com/watch?v=7WEd34oW9BI.
[161] Here it is important to note that the U.S. and the EU consider the ELN to be a terrorist organization; as of this writing, Duque has come close to recognizing them as "terrorist" organization, and thereby making them an illegitimate actor for whom a peace process is not an option.
[162] Simons, G. "Fourth Generation Warfare and The Clash of Civilizations." *Journal of Islamic Studies* 21, no. 3 (2010), 391-412. doi:10.1093/jis/etq042, p. 393.

operationalizing them; the overarching premises can be lost in the minutia, and in the moment. The idea of an insurgent meeting his or her enemy, just like the COIN or SOF member on the ground in a community trying to win hearts and minds (HAM) is going to be different in reality than it was in theory; it is visceral, real, personal, and, again, going back to Kalyvas, intimate. And this is what lingers, if one doesn't shut off his or her humanity in the process. Some try, but on the fundamental level of guerrilla warfare and insurgencies, to do so is to lose touch with the goal, and thereby, lose the initiative. In both Stability and Support Operations (SASO) (which is how the U.S., for instance, has been primarily engaged with Colombia's military) and COIN (in which the U.S. gives training), the point is to target the insurgency and its leaders while also winning hearts and minds (HAM), meaning, in the most effective sense, to inherently trigger the intimate for purposes of trust.

However, if looking from the macro perspective, this is not the tack that the U.S. government, including in theorizing COIN from the higher levels, has often taken. The analysis and promulgation of COIN on a strategic level, for instance, by Austin Long for RAND, reflects the McKenzie tendencies that have persisted, especially in the upper ranks, eschewing ground-level visceral reality by making it into a solely logical, intellectual exercise, and in broad terms:

> The answer was to restore the hope of the people and gain their support for the government. In order to do this, COIN would consist of providing the people security from the predations by government and insurgent forces and reducing the negative consequences of development while enhancing positive aspects. Increasing political rights of the people, improving standards of living, and reducing

corruption and abuse of government power were key prescriptions of this COIN theory.[163]

This overarching series of ultra-logical components, however, *again* would still need to be operationalized on the ground—meaning it would be—ostensibly—someone else's problem down the chain of command. However, it was the primary premise of HAM, originating with the British in Malaya and adopted for Vietnam and other asymmetric conflicts by the U.S., which as with the British, given an often imperialist tone, came with questionable success. This would be followed later by other theories by subsequent think tanks like RAND, such as the "cost/benefit, or coercion, theory"—meant to utilize systems theory and "econometric techniques"—and according to such a systems analysis, "all COIN efforts [would] be evaluated in terms of how well they either raised the cost of inputs to the system or interfered with outputs."[164] Further: "Populations were viewed as rational actors that would respond in more or less predictable ways to incentives and sanctions from the competing systems of insurgent and counterinsurgent."[165]

And:

> "Many authors regard economic growth as one of the criteria for winning. This is not listed here as necessary, though in most cases some economic betterment of people is necessary for popular support of government and its programs...Popular support helps develop a government or contributes to its viability, but it may not be a necessary condition"[166].

---

[163] Long, Austin. "What are insurgencies and how does one fight them?" In *On "Other War": Lessons from Five Decades of RAND Counterinsurgency Research*, 21-32. Santa Monica: Rand Corporation, 2006, p. 25.
[164] Ibid., p. 25.
[165] Ibid..
[166] Ibid., p. 26.

In other words, one can surmise that all people should be logical, even in war; if these processes don't work, sheer developed world force might indeed be an alternative. Those affected by such insurgencies and asymmetric engagement are to be factored in as data, rather than flesh and blood communities. Imagine, then, when doing COIN analysis, that one would have a "ratcheted escalation problem" in which "'negative feelings' are irrelevant; it is negative actions that matter"—the "COIN force would be trapped by the ratchet, having escalated but unable to make the final repressive effort needed to quell the insurgency."[167] This "cost/benefit' theory via a systems lens therefore naturally "assumed the population to be completely indifferent to insurgent and counterinsurgent, so whichever side provided the better set of incentives and disincentives would prevail."[168]

Indeed, the insights about ground-level reality, including the actual human beings involved, their interests, their history, loyalties, experiences, and emotions—essential to consider in this kind of warfare—which even Clausewitz recognized—in this view, be damned. However, as this is also the perspective that has been involved in U.S. support of Colombia, including via law enforcement and advisory capacity for the Colombian military, it becomes inordinately relevant. In going back to the "agrarian peasant" perspective which is susceptible to the ideas and presence of an insurgency, if one is a *Campesino*, the reality is going to be the accepted wisdom of elites supported by the Colombian state, and hence its military and non-state but illicitly state-sanctioned paramilitaries, often working with narco-syndicates in a corrupt cycle of mutual benefit, while insurgencies continue their operations—whether following their ideological foundations rather than flouting them. In

---

[167] Ibid., p. 28.
[168] Ibid., p. 30.

each case, each of these respective groups has its own interests, but which, however, invariably affects the communities whom all parties are, in one way or another, purportedly serving.

Colombia, the ELN, and the United States to 2017

And it is here that one gets into the reality of Colombia, as it has been, in moving forward in time from the 1960's and the ELN's inception, to the 1970's and 80's to the present. This includes not only foreign involvements by the U.S. with law enforcement, military hardware, and training, but also via varying peace processes with respective Demobilization, Disarmament, Reintegration (DDR) efforts among various non-state armed groups. Glaringly apparent, and to Colombians' detriment, is the failure of such efforts, while criminal activity rises, both within the state and often tangential to it, both via corruption and the rise of criminal and narco-syndicates (BACRIM) that often involve state actors as well as members of illicit groups. Amidst this cacophony of varying, and often criminal interests, there has been a lapse in the strict maintenance of any foundational ideology, whether for benefit—and/or for survival.

From the perspective of the United States, this has been, internationally, about international supremacy, first in a Cold War, bi-polar stance against the Soviet Union, which instigated proxy conflicts, including in Latin America; after the end of the Cold War, it would be to maintain status as a unipolar power, despite the increasing presence of "fragile" and "failed" states,[169] with other larger and increasingly powerful international actors, such as India, Russia, and China jockeying for position, including in the two latter cases, exerting international influence via arms and aid in return for certain inducements, including resource rights. The developed world was seeing "increased levels of

---

[169] Bunker, p. 2.

criminality, extremism, terrorism, and barbarism taking place," along with "new forms of insurgency emerging".[170] Following 9/11, this emphasis on the threat of insurgencies, and particularly in first the Middle East, and then in North Africa (combined: MENA), often took away any focus on other areas, though depending upon what power might be at work, the vigilance necessary to keep an eye on several balls in the air could only be an overwhelming objective.

It was during this time that the U.S. and its allies developed newer terms, including for indications and warnings (I&W), when it came to any such threat. When it came to insurgencies, a more formalized term developed; from the U.S. Army's Strategic Studies Institute (SSI), for instance, the May 2014 Field Manual (FM) 3-24, under "Insurgencies and Counterinsurgencies": "...the organized use of subversion and violence to seize, nullify, or challenge political control of a region. Insurgency can also refer to the group itself".[171] As Bunker points out, "both elements of subversion and violence are required to characterize an insurgency."[172] Subversion alone, "derived from co-option and corruption" can be seen from criminal elements, including political actors within the state or organized crime, usually using "minimal levels of criminal violence."[173] When a non-state, organized force uses violence via conventional military strategies for political—and not just criminal—purposes, that is where the "insurgency" label would kick in.[174]

Here, too, a draft of FM 3-4 also further defined "political control" as "a system of government or existing social order" that could be subverted when "overthrown,

---

[170] Ibid..
[171] Bunker, p.3.
[172] Ibid..
[173] Ibid., p.p. 3-4.
[174] Ibid., p. 4.

changed, or undermined".[175] Bunker here, in this SSI document, also gets into an understanding of the state itself, in case its own definition might be unclear: it is the "strategic prize being targeted by an insurgent force" with "sovereign rights" "within a physical (human) space" being made up of the following: "a) ideology; b) government; c) economy; d) military; e) populace; and f) religion (in a secularized context) and the ensuing relationships that exist between them."[176] He goes even further, once again invoking Clausewitz via "Clausewitzian thinking" regarding the "Westphalian state" in its older usage being the "dominant form of social and political organization"; though this, he suggests, can be updated into the current "liberal democratic" and more "modernist" definition, which is suggested by a "strong middle class, upward social mobility, a separation of church and state, the enfranchisement of women [and] personal liberties" as "enshrined in the Bill of Rights and Constitution"—which is "the most preferable and legitimate form of the Westphalian state."[177] His caution, however, is that this is from an inherently Western bias; "derived from this orientation, the solution to the threat of insurgency is the development of state and societal institutions so that they resemble Western liberal democratic states and cultures" which similar to the RAND playbook on COIN and HAM might smack of a certain ethnocentrism.[178] This is, he recognizes, however, the perspective of "modern Army counterinsurgency (COIN) doctrine"—"solidly Western state centric in orientation" which has "both benefited and suffered as a result".[179]

In approaching Colombia, ostensibly from the perspective of Stability and Support Operations (SASO),

---

[175] Ibid..
[176] Ibid..
[177] Ibid..
[178] Ibid., p.p. 5-6.
[179] Ibid., p.6.

law enforcement, and training in COIN, elements of terrorism are inherently in the mix, given the armed violence and the terrorist acts committed by both narco-syndicates and non-state armed actors.[180] Here the I&W thinking, from 2001 on, derived from a foundation in David Rapoport's "four waves" theory; each "wave" encompassed 40-45 years (give or take) and were generally precipitated by a particular event.[181] First was anarchism, from the 1880's to the 1920's to "bring about the destruction of government and to liberate individuals from the shackles of artificial human convention"; second was anti-colonial, or nationalistic, from the 1920's to the 1960's; the third wave was the "new-left" from the late 1960's – 90's; and the fourth wave is based on "religious extremism" which is "predominantly Islamic" and "started in 1979" while being "expected to continue out to about 2020 to 2025."[182]

The important point here is the distinct inclusion of *narcocultura*, which began in the late 1970's and continues to exist, first in the rise of the Medellin and Cali cartels in Colombia, but then included the nexus among Mexico, Panama, other connected states and non-state armed groups or insurgencies, to the point where the edges blur. The social, economic, political and security elements combine to form a sort of hybrid, utilizing both insurgency and terrorist organization capacities—enough so that terrorist, insurgency, and those studying trans-national international crime are now seeing "convergence"[183] in a way that those on the ground have seen for some time and take as rather obvious and undisputed fact. This has been suggested as creating a new form of "commercial insurgency" typology,

---

[180] Even if the particular group is not officially, per official definition, "terrorist" which requires unlawful use of violence for a particular religious, ideological, or political objective.
[181] Ibid., p. 7.
[182] Ibid., p.p. 7-8.
[183] Ibid., p. 10.

which can be characterized by a "widespread and sustained criminal activity with a proto-political dimension that challenges the security of the state" and in terms of *narcocultura*, is manifested as "narco-insurgency" so that its "defining feature is expansion of the criminal activity into a security threat, especially in the hinterlands where government control is limited."[184]

It is into this world that the ELN—like FARC, ELP, M-19, and the state-backed Colombian paramilitaries—were thrust during this time period. At the same time were international interests that bombarded Colombia with offers of aid and development to enter more into the international market for its goods, providing infrastructure and inducements, including to get illicit groups under control. At the same time, given to whom such inducements would inevitably be going as they had before, the urban Left began to push a "rising tide of mobilization" in terms of protests, at first regarding conditions and opportunity for union workers as more moved into the cities, but later, involving the corruption of the state itself. By 1973, 59.5% of over 23 million Colombians were living in cities, and the need for work became endemic.[185] As students, trade unions, etc., became more powerful, "the great civil strike"—*paro civico*—of 1977 occurred, which ostensibly shut down the cities and "paralyzed the country." According to Hylton:

> The strike was repressed with great violence, as civil rights and the rule of law were suspended and followed by a dirty war against the Left and its constituents; this marked the beginning of widespread torture and forced disappearances... Connected to military intelligence, death squads and paramilitaries proliferated. The draconian Security

---

[184] Ibid., p. 11.
[185] Hylton, Forrest. "The Experience of Defeat." *Historical Materialism* 22, no. 1 (2014), 67-104. doi:10.1163/1569206x-12341335, p. 84.

Statute implemented under Liberal President Julio Cesar Turbay Ayala and General Camacho Leyva in 1978 marked a watershed, since civilian authority gave way to military authority on all matters related to public order.[186]

The thought was, among the left, that this was the precursor to a "nationwide insurrection" as had happened to spark *La Violencia;* FARC added "EP" to their name, M-19 rose in the ranks, and the Colombian state and associated paramilitaries countered, creating almost apocalyptic violence, as it seemed all parties were hell bent on "destroy[ing] the country in order to save it.[187]

For the ELN, this was a time of unprecedented growth not only ideologically, but economically. Almost decimated in the early 70's to the smallest numbers, by the 1980's, ELN "grew faster than any other insurgent organization".[188] While FARC had entered into the cocaine business to fill its coffers, given that coca production was "centered in FARC territory," the ELN instead chose to take advantage of the multinational conglomerates with their endless capital; as coffee and national manufacturing were protected, "bananas, coal, gold, and petroleum...offered new opportunities" via establishing "protection rackets and extract rents".[189] As the ELN had "pioneered the strategy,"[190] it profited the most from it. Also at this point, the ELN also began expanding to what it considered its "urban front" among students and the "urban Left".[191] With violence only continuing in all fronts—the cities and the rural areas—the criminal enterprises rose, including among

---

[186] Ibid., p.p. 84-5.
[187] Ibid., p. 46
[188] Ibid., p. 86.
[189] Ibid..
[190] Ibid..
[191] Ibid..

the narco-syndicates, representing the rise of the Colombian cartels. Bringing in vast sums of cash from which to buy off public officials, making deals with paramilitaries to either ignore or assist in trafficking (which was also the case with FARC in its respective territories), as Hylton puts it, Colombia became "more rigidly exclusive, unequal, and unjust" embodied by the same

> ...historic blocs of landlords, licit and illicit entrepreneurs, active and retired military and police officers [on the take], local and national machine politicians, layers of middle and working classes, and the lumpenproletariat as well as the *lumpenbourgeoisie*—the latter two class factions tied to death squads and organized crime.[192]

And as the Cold War ended, with the Soviet Union no longer funding FARC, it immersed itself even further into the drug and other illicit trade, which only spurred the United States to continue to pump money into Colombian law enforcement efforts; as Hylton suggests, this was lucrative enough that even the Colombian government didn't do as much as it could have, for as long as narco-trafficking and insurgencies existed, "large amounts of US and Colombian aid would continue to flow into the coffers of the armed forces [which included the national police], no matter how inept counter-insurgent efforts might be."[193]

It was at this point when the ELN, by the 1990's, in having successfully rebuilt itself, and having established itself in resource-rich areas in which extortion rackets, kidnap and ransom (K&R) known as "miracle fishing" or *pescas milagrosas,*[194] and illicit taxes were levied to

---

[192] Ibid., p. 89.
[193] Ibid..
[194] Tompkins & Newton, p. 194

maintain economic flow, the ELN command structure set three explicit goals for the insurgency:

- To "expand its finances as well as its capacity of military troops in order to achieve the status of a major political actor among Colombia's potent assortment of belligerents";
- To secure a "piece of territory under its own [total] control" a—*zona de despeje*-- which "became the group's most enunciated objective";
- To "influence a restructuring of the Colombian political economy consistent with their ideological premises."[195]

The final point to the three was not to be dismissed; their ideological and liberation theological objectives were absolute enough to "plan how to bring about consciousness during agitation."[196] According to Tompkins and Newton, in quoting from among the ELN cadre:

> It was the epoch of writing handbooks, talks, envisioning with the masses what could be created... We even started to make extraordinary things, like completing sociological research in areas, characterizing local communities, their problems, contradictions...[197]

Also important was the reverence for leadership, with almost a religious devotion. Vasquez, Torres, and Perez became almost "mythical figures"—with their histories known by all among the ELN *frentes.*[198]. Torres, especially, in having brought the liberation theological component to the insurgency caused him to be revered, even when he was defrocked as a priest because of "his political activism" it

---

[195] Ibid., p. 181.
[196] Ibid..
[197] Ibid., p. 182.
[198] Ibid., p. 185.

"did not impact his reputation, and his popularity continued to grow throughout Colombia."[199] According to one ELN member:

> In language that echoed the gospels Torres said that revolution was "the way to bring about a government that feeds the hungry, clothes the naked, teaches the ignorant, puts into practice the works of charity, and love for neighbor, not just every now and then, and not just for a few, but for the majority of our neighbors."[200]

Perez, the Spanish priest who was "deeply inspired by Torres' commitment to the ELN and the call to revolution" ended up leading the ELN from 1973-1998.[201] It was in 1998 that the ELN's leadership was taken by Nicolas Rodriguez Bautista, *nomme de guerre* "Gambino," who had been a "peasant recruit" in 1964[202] and rose in the ranks to continue to lead it until just before this book's publication in 2021. The notion of lifelong commitment to the organization remains deeply ingrained in the ELN; those who joined then, as now, are indoctrinated into notions of loyalty and that the ELN's revolution is one "of a long line of honorable struggles" to which when Bautista, according to an anecdote, had told his father he was going to officially join "Vasquez and his guerrillas," his father had imparted his own belief from the time of *La Violencia:*

> If you decide to struggle, you must be faithful until the death. Victory is not just turning the corner. If you decide to struggle, that becomes your life. It is not like in a movie, it won't be easy. In this struggle there are not heroes that come, fight, vanquish and

---

[199] Ibid..
[200] Ibid..
[201] Ibid..
[202] Ibid..

then return home... The struggle is for the rest of your life.[203]

What is important to understand here is that like any movement—or any insurgency—especially one based on strong, ideological foundations, is that the psychological, historical, and sociological components are essential; they cannot be separated from the whole and they act as a counter to any questioning of particular acts, including what may be deemed as "legitimate"—including acts of insurgent violence. Given the experiences of Colombians, especially in rural areas of the time, often separated by hours on bad roads or paths to any village or larger community, amidst vast poverty, state-sponsored violence, and rapt insecurity, one is going to find security wherever it can be found. As Simons suggests:

> For all practical purposes, reality is what people perceive it to be and that is what they tend to act on or can be persuaded to act on. Accordingly, a great deal of effort goes into cultivating particular perceptions of reality so that an agenda that, under other circumstances, might not be acceptable to people, comes to be perceived by those people as their only salvation.[204]

It is not difficult to imagine, given the conditions from the *La Violencia* to the 1960's, and the brutal government-sponsored violence during the 1980's in one form or another to the present, any peace process or cease fire ultimately unsuccessful because of a lack of trust and incapacity to back promises with concerted action,[205] that

---

[203] Ibid., p. 187.
[204] Simons, p. 393.
[205] Here, I consider the rapidly deteriorating peace with FARC under Duque as heading in that distinct direction.

dissatisfaction in the best case scenario and abject poverty and fear in the worst would be impetus enough to consider where such security might be found, and certain perceptions galvanized.

In the meantime, by 2000, under the Clinton administration, the United States had definitively "stepped in" and backed the counterinsurgent "Right"—meaning the Colombian government—via "advanced training, high-tech weaponry, and communications commitment" with four-fifths of an "initial $1.3 billion in US government aid" going to the police and armed forces, in which anything but the high-tech aspects "of which the US was in charge," and "the principal means of waging counterinsurgency was to link the civilian population to the armed forces through intelligence networks and paramilitary militias"—which, incidentally, "control[ed] the country's most lucrative cocaine export routes, as well as local and regional office[s]".[206] The paramilitary, by 2002, "occupied one-third of congressional seats" and by 2006 "won 22 out of 32 departmental governorships".[207] They also controlled by 2007 5.5 million hectares of land, usurping former landowners with money derived for "security" from Plan Colombia, while these "rural areas lacked adequate schools, health clinics, passable roads, functioning sewage systems, or adequate housing"; aid for development or for peace and justice initiatives "received less than five percent" of Plan Colombia's budget, while between "2000-2010, the military budget tripled, and Colombia had the world's third-largest fleet of helicopters".[208] At the same time, Colombia continued to be a "cocaine republic" and "Colombian elites" continued to be "among the most violent and criminal in the hemisphere".[209]

---

[206] Hylton, p.p. 90-91.
[207] Ibid., p. 91.
[208] Ibid..
[209] Ibid, p. 94.

While the ELN continued to remain in remote areas outside of the Colombian government's control—which again, like with FARC—as long as they existed, they remained a reason to convince developed countries to either fund counter-narcotics/counterinsurgency actions, or later, also lucrative peace processes—it also expanded its intelligence and social mobilization capacities into urban areas, where *urbanos,* or the National Urban War Front [FGUN in Spanish] "provide[s] support, gather[s] intelligence, and serve[s] as community organizers."[210] As Tompkins and Newton note, "these urbanos could have transitioned into the armed component of the ELN, but to become a soldier required proving oneself to the rural guerrilla front"; it also provided a valuable set of assets to be able to have operators on the outside.[211] Some would have public capacities, "producing newspapers, writing editorials" and distributing manifestos and "other propaganda materials to be distributed".[212]

In the rural fronts, new ELN members, once proving themselves, would continue, as they had at the inception of the insurgency, to be indoctrinated via ritual (including, when fully indoctrinated, their *nomme de guerre)*, drills, education and daily courses "varying from literacy to the martyr history of the ELN, specifically regarding Torres", with the armed component swearing "an unbreakable vow of compliance," and as with any military, "higher levels of solidarity because they had to trust each other with their lives".[213]

In terms of its authority, "the group has incontrovertible de facto rule in the areas where it operates, from which it launches sustained guerrilla warfare such as

[210] Tompkins & Newton, p. 187.
[211] Ibid., p. 188.
[212] Ibid., p. 189.
[213] Ibid..

ambushes, sniper shootings, attacks with a variety of explosives and gas and oil pipeline bombings" affecting "118 (or one in ten) municipalities" with six regional war fronts, themselves divided into 29 rural fronts and 22 companies. On the practical, and political side, political actions—including those considered "terrorist"—have involved threats of bombings, bombings, particularly of the power grid and oil pipelines, in addition to the high-profile kidnappings.[214]

Last but not least, in terms of any peace process: FARC, and its experiences, has continued to be a cautionary tale for the ELN. While the ELN has engaged in cease fires (including the 100 day cease fire between October 2017 and January 2018), and has maintained that it would attend peace processes if trust could be established, there were no realistic considerations regarding any significant peace until 2014, when there were talks, held in secret, regarding "defining an agenda".[215] In March 2016, talking points were released, including, 1) Participation of Society in Peace-Building; 2) Democracy for Peace; 3) Transformations for Peace; 4) Victims; 5) End of the Conflict; and 6) Implementation.[216] The broad nature of the subjects caused there to be friction, along with the Colombian government demanding the release of all kidnapping victims; "after months of mutual public recriminations" the last kidnapping victim was released on February 2, 2017, after which "[f]ormal talks began five days later".[217] The only thing upon which the parties agreed was the "creation of a Group of Supporting, Accompanying, and Cooperating Countries," comprising

---

[214] Ibid., p. 196.
[215] "The Missing Peace: Colombia's New Government and Last Guerrillas." Crisis Group. Last modified July 12, 2018. https://www.crisisgroup.org/latin-america-caribbean/andes/colombia/68-missing-peace-colombias-new-government-and-last-guerrillas, p. 15.
[216] Ibid., p.p. 15-16.
[217] Ibid., p. 16.

Germany, the Netherlands, Italy, Switzerland, and Sweden who would "aid the process politically, technically, and financially.[218] Brazil, Chile, Cuba, Norway, and Venezuela are "guarantors" who "attend the negotiations when in session and can host the talks if need be".[219]

In the interim, FARC indeed formalized peace in 2016 with Colombian government in its own process, going through an unsuccessful referendum among the public (terms not acceptable to many victims of FARC violence having been what had been perceived as any form of amnesty from crimes), later to have the agreement revised and passed by both houses of the Colombian legislature,[220] with the federal judiciary signing off on the agreement, including to abide by international law.[221]

---

[218] Ibid..

[219] Ibid..

[220] "Why Colombians Distrust the FARC Peace Deal." The Economist. Last modified May 24, 2018. https://www.economist.com/the-economist-explains/2018/05/24/why-colombians-distrust-the-farc-peace-deal.

[221] Alvira, Gustavo. "Toward a New Amnesty:The Colombian Peace Process and the Inter-American Court of Human Rights." *Tulane Journal of International and Comparative Law* 22 (2013), 119-144. https://heinonline.org, p. 130.

Part III: A Brewing Storm:

The United States, Colombia, ELN, and the Implications of the Venezuelan Crisis—2018 to the Present

Precursor to the Storm

2018 was a seminal year for the ELN, not just in terms of Ivan Duque's election and the vulnerabilities of the FARC peace process coming to light, but in terms of sudden revelations about the ELN's activities not just in Colombia, but in neighboring and adjacent states, including Ecuador, Brazil, Guyana, Suriname, and Panama. As the International Crisis Group (ICG) noted in their July 2018 report on the ELN, "the ELN stands out for its resilience in modern-day Colombia...Because of its clandestine operations and small military branch in comparison to that of the FARC, the ELN remains a mystery to many Colombians."[222] This is true except in the areas where the ELN operates, though the ICG recognizes that part of the ELN's covert nature—and the inaccessibility of its Central Command—is bolstered, too, by those under cover, including "civilian members, who may be plainclothes fighters leading normal lives but lend support to the guerrillas when need be, through violent actions, intelligence gathering or coercive political control. Others are activists who 'insert' themselves into grassroots and political movements".[223] This iteration of ELN includes such "civilians" growing faster than the military cadres, as such "growth is at the request of local communities who either seek protection from alleged paramilitaries' incursions or who simply support the guerrillas."[224] Further, as the *frentes* and the units within them "carry out decisions with a high degree of autonomy"[225] based on the command structure of the organization, outside of instances in which, such as "in Arauca and Cauca, appear to have placed representatives inside local governments or...enjoy direct relationships with officials",[226] intelligence on the ELN is difficult to obtain.

---

[222] ICG "The Missing Peace", p. 3.
[223] Ibid., p. 5.
[224] Ibid..
[225] Ibid., p. 6.
[226] Ibid..

This is, in fact, purposeful. Unlike FARC who had made a usual practice of being front and center amidst the press, especially during the peace process, ELN continued in its guerrilla *foco* tactics; it has taken advantage of the "complex terrain" by hiding numbers and resources. As Rod Thornton points out, "[a]s with any asymmetric warrior, the lower the profile that can be developed, the less likely [they] are to show up on the 'radar' of their more powerful state opponents."[227] The ELN has utilized this strategy on a fundamental level to the present, and what Thornton uses to describe a terrorist cell can be interpolated in terms of the ELN units and *frentes*: "loose associations" that are "lighter, more flexible, and self-contained".[228] This, however, while it may have been a disconcerting realization among Western military when approaching Daesh and AQ in MENA, this is exactly the kind of operational environment in which the ELN has operated for over 50 years. They have only continued to operate on the basis of "expansion and regional consolidation" as well as taking pointed, dramatic actions when feeling the need to respond to Colombia's state apparatus. In some cases, however, a *frente*'s action backfires from its objective, such as in the case of the Barranquilla police station bombing in January 2018 by the National Urban War Front, killing seven officers and wounding 40, causing a backlash and a detrimental effect in the public's perception of the ELN as a whole.[229]

The additional concern regarding the ELN's public perception, and also perhaps influenced by the more "self-contained" nature of the fronts is the foray into "coca production and cocaine trafficking, despite an internal prohibition on doing so."[230] Unlike FARC, the ELN had for

---

[227] Thornton, p. 31.
[228] Ibid..
[229] ICG, "The Missing Peace", p. 8.
[230] Ibid., p. 9.

most of its history made a point to not dive headfirst into narco-trafficking, given that their aim was to target the Colombian state, including its elites, and Western multi-national conglomerates. However, as FARC gave up territory and influence with its peace process, there was more incentive to pick up the slack, including as a means of countering the newly-reinvigorated paramilitaries.

Also of concern is the "generational transition" from the old guard to the new, in which "many of its younger leaders appear more interested in keeping local power and the economic benefits";[231] whereas the ICG references this in terms of any possible peace process, this also may mean—and significantly—that such generations could be less directly influenced by the original ideological and theological foundations as time goes on. With continued opportunity, including in Venezuela and elsewhere, the temptation to dive into a more distinctly criminal identity rather than maintaining that of the original insurgency is a distinct possibility. Until such is proven, however, the ELN, under "Gambino" until mid-2021 (having gone to Cuba for peace talks, having remained because of arrest risk[232]) still maintained its overarching philosophy, including among Command; this has contributed to certain fronts making a point to engage civil society, including in some areas with the local governments. They have held meetings with citizens to hear grievances, have eschewed renewed efforts for peace processes as long as "social and humanitarian" issues aren't given primacy, and some in rural areas have hoped it would not disarm, in that they are protection against paramilitaries, as well as those, such as one community leader in ELN territory, who believe it to be a "'necessary

[231] Ibid., p. 10
[232] "Colombia's ELN Rebel Leaders Say They Will Not Leave Cuba." U.S. Last modified January 31, 2019. https://www.reuters.com/article/us-colombia-rebels/colombias-eln-rebel-leaders-say-they-will-not-leave-cuba-idUSKCN1PP2V5.

evil,' because without them the thieves and rapists would 'invade' her town."[233] Such towns in ELN territory are hampered by their remote location and the lack of services provided by the state, including "no running water" certain areas where "electricity is rationed" and "comes on only for a few hours in the evening".[234] Such locations, knowing that they are caught between the ELN and the state, can often "express reluctant sympathy for the guerrillas' cause, as well as a deep-rooted fear" with one resident saying, "We're poor and so these guys are the only ones who can help us. But we know they're not our real friends."[235] In even thinking about any peace process, those in rural communities whom it would most affect are also not impressed by what they have seen with FARC, including dissidents who instead of embracing any ideological insurgency, instead transformed into criminal armies intent on creating their own cocaine monopolies: "With the [FARC] peace process, we expected schools and hospitals to be built. But all we got is more violence…[i]f peace with FARC brought us more war, what will peace with the ELN bring us?"[236]

In terms of the peace process with the ELN, as of this writing, it has ostensibly ended; the significant development of the cease fire of 100 days between October 2017 and January 2018 was not renewed, given "ELN perceptions that the government was violating the ceasefire" with alleged state-sponsored murders by police in ELN territory, including of community leaders, while also attempting to "seize territory under ELN control".[237] The government

---

[233] ICG, "The Missing Peace", p. 11.
[234] "As Peace Talks Flail, Colombia's ELN Seeks 'Liberation or Death'."
InSight Crime. Last modified October 10, 2018.
https://www.insightcrime.org/news/analysis/peace-talks-flail-colombias-eln-seeks-liberation-death/.
[235] Ibid..
[236] Ibid..
[237] ICG, "The Missing Peace", p. 17.

countered, claiming the right to "fight crime anywhere in the country".[238] This, for the ELN, was consistent with their argument why past peace negotiations have stalled and failed, calling such excuses "perfidy" while in this particular case "the government had played 'judge and jury'"— including "by impeding any real verification of alleged ceasefire violations" committed by Colombian security forces.[239] And, subsequent to these allegations, came the Barranquilla attack. Any later attempts to re-ignite talks, including in Quito, Ecuador, stalled when they were halted by Ecuadorian President Lenin Moreno in "retaliation against the Colombian government for providing what Quito viewed as insufficient help in the case of the kidnapping and murder of two journalists and their driver by FARC dissidents operating in both countries".[240] ELN has consistently reiterated that FARC "negotiated a bad deal," with one ELN officer, *nomme de guerre* "Estacio," saying that "They sold out everything they believed in. The government made a fool of them. We won't fall for that."[241] Another, a commander from the Western War Front, "Uriel," said, "We've told the government before…[i]f they want to get rid of the guerrilla, then they need to get rid of the reasons for which we exist."[242] Until then, the ELN's daily routine will continue, which among the military wing, includes:

> 6am inspection, followed by classes in current affairs, Marxist ideology, and explosives training. The afternoon is devoted to military exercise. The day ends at 6pm with another inspection and the singing of the ELN anthem, which includes a

---

[238] Ibid..
[239] Ibid..
[240] Ibid., p. 18.
[241] "As Peace Talks Fail," p.1.
[242] Ibid..

repetition of the lyrics, "Not one step back! Liberation or death!"[243]

Ivan Duque's election indeed only added to the distrust between the ELN and the Colombian government; he has been known as a hard-liner regarding the peace process in comparison to Juan Miguel Santos, the outgoing Colombian President who had presided over the FARC peace process enough to win the Nobel Peace Prize.[244] In the past, Duque has labeled the ELN as "terrorists", and he "campaigned proposing a strict series of preconditions for talks" including that "negotiations would cover only the [DDR] process" and "not the movement's political demands".[245] As the ICG notes in their May 2018 report, "Duque's conditions would spell the end of peace talks. The ELN flatly rejects any proposal by what it sees as the Colombian elite aimed at demobilizing the group without any political reform in return".[246]

Given that the FARC peace process has been less than successful, with such growing dissent among the ranks of demobilized FARC and the presence and growing number of FARC dissenters either creating their own fronts or joining, in some cases, and/or allying with the ELN, with the ELN's growing presence in Venezuela and other surrounding states, including Ecuador and now with proof of their incursion into Guyana and Brazil, there is not much incentive, given Duque's rabid intransigence, to capitulate. This intransigence was further strengthened by the ELN taking responsibility for the January 17, 2019 car bombing, of the General Santander police academy that left 21 dead

---

[243] Ibid..

[244] "The Nobel Peace Prize 2016." NobelPrize.org. Accessed April 12, 2019. https://www.nobelprize.org/prizes/peace/2016/santos/facts/.

[245] ICG, "The Missing Peace", p. 18.

[246] Ibid..

and 68 wounded.[247] The reason: "a Colombian military bombing on one of [ELN's] bases during a unilateral ceasefire in late December 2018" which breached a Christmas cease-fire".[248]

The Current Operational Environment of the ELN

At the moment, when it comes to Colombian security, and the nuances involved regarding the ELN, it is impossible not to examine the influence of the crisis in Venezuela, and its contribution to the lack of both regional security, and the involvement of the United States, along with other developed powers. This also brings in the discussions of international criminal elements, given that such crises are conducive to their operations in taking advantage of the proverbial chaos. This includes not just narco-trafficking (given Colombia produces 80% of the world's cocaine[249]), but weapons trafficking for both criminal and insurgent elements, economic impacts including money laundering, the involvement of illicit resource trade (minerals such a coltan, gold, uranium, etc.), oil, coal, etc., and then the effects upon the communities in which such criminality has its most profound impact. That the ELN is immersed in this reality is not a surprise; again, given the generational shift, dissolving peace, hardline political posturing from both the right (Duque in Colombia) and the left (Maduro in Venezuela), and vast movement of Venezuelan citizens escaping into surrounding countries, Colombia included, it has provided an opportunity for the

---

[247] "The ELN's Attack on the National Police Academy in Bogotá and Its Implications – Combating Terrorism Center at West Point." Combating Terrorism Center at West Point. Last modified March 4, 2019.
https://ctc.usma.edu/elns-attack-national-police-academy-bogota-implications/.
[248] Ibid..
[249] Casa Editorial El Tiempo. "Colombia, 40 Años Atrapada En El Negocio Del Tráfico De Cocaína." El Tiempo. Last modified April 11, 2019.
https://www.eltiempo.com/justicia/conflicto-y-narcotrafico/como-ha-sido-el-negocio-del-trafico-de-coca-en-colombia-348756.

ELN to both expand and flourish, establishing footholds that had, per their capacity and insurgent strategy, remained under the radar among the international public until recently, when varying crises brought their current involvements to more public attention. Given, too, that the Trump administration at one point seemed to choose Venezuela as a hill on which to potentially assert 21st Century hemispheric primacy, as the Russians and Chinese also sought to take advantage of Venezuelan chaos, again, as mentioned at the beginning of Part III, the possibility of a perfect storm continued to become more and more relevant.

First, and because it's the most recognizable behemoth, is the cocaine industry, which feeds into illicit trafficking, money laundering, and much else, including in transportation, utilizing similar routes across insurgent territory, especially with the FARC contingents which capitulated to the peace agreement having demobilized. By last estimate, Colombia produced 921 metric tons of cocaine in 2017 from 209,000 hectares of coca crops.[250] Former Colombian President Santos had committed to eradicating 180,000 hectares by 2023, with current President Duque facing 80% of that promise left to be implemented.[251] Part of the FARC peace process also was supposed to create a substitution program for illegal crops—coca among them—that was been stymied by government, paramilitaries as *Bandas Criminales* (BACRIM), and FARC dissidents.[252] Coca farmers had been promised US$300 a month, plus "additional benefits" such as "technical assistance to help

---

[250] "Colombia President Duque's 5 'Hot Potatoes'." InSight Crime. Last modified August 8, 2018.
https://www.insightcrime.org/news/analysis/colombia-president-duque-5-hot-potatoes/.
[251] Ibid..
[252] "Briefing: Needs Mount in Colombia As Peace Commitments Lag." The New Humanitarian. Last modified April 4, 2019.
https://www.thenewhumanitarian.org/analysis/2019/03/25/briefing-needs-mount-colombia-peace-commitments-lag.

them grow and sell legal produce"; however, while "close to 100,000 coca-growing families agreed to take part" though no assistance has been, in most cases, forthcoming to the levels promised.[253] As Kyle Johnson from ICG suggested, "If crop substitution fails to give [C]ampesinos a sustainable livelihood...most, if not all, will go back to growing coca."[254]   This has proven to be the case, with environmentalists in Colombia pointing to Duque's use of poisonous glyphosates to eradicate coca crops. To add further difficulty to an already dire situation, 400 community leaders, "most of them crop substitution advocates," as of April 2019, had been murdered.[255] This has only continued. A number of the culprits are former FARC or AUC (now BACRIM), who either never entered—or chose to leave— the DDR process. In not having felt any guarantee of success in the reintegration process, the thought perhaps turned to: "it is therefore better to join the dissidents".[256]

Add to this vast corruption within the Colombian government, including greater sophistication from "years of collusion with criminal actors" to the point where some government officials have "establish[ed] their own criminal organizations within state institutions," including—in one case—a corruption network, "Cartel de la Toga," within the Supreme Court, in which the main prosecutor in charge of corruption investigations was actually at the center of the criminal enterprise.[257] The situation in Colombia, whether in urban or rural environments, has become so immersed in such activity that "corruption is seen as a legitimate way to build consensus and make government work, especially in

---

[253] Ibid..
[254] Ibid..
[255] Ibid..
[256] Ibid..
[257] Ibid..

regions where local political actors and criminal actors intermingle."[258]

Additionally, and as has been stated throughout, many government officials are directly connected to the paramilitaries, who are directly associated with the drug trade; the former umbrella organization of paramilitary forces aligned with the state, the *Autodefensas Unidas de Colombia* (AUC), had been demobilized, at least officially, by 2005, having signed the agreement in 2003.[259] According to Saab and Taylor, "In return the government promised to suspend arrest warrants...and to limit criminal prosecution and extradition of ex-combatants, concessions which were later codified in the Peace and Justice Law (Law 975) in July 2005 that was subsequently struck down, while its terms still remained intact."[260] This only allowed members of such groups to not openly demobilize and instead "transition" into BACRIM: "more informal emerging criminal bands"[261]. They, however, did not lose their association with state officials, or the elites; according to *Le Figaro*, these groups have been said to control 40% of cocaine exports out of Colombia.[262] The drug trade is widely considered to be larger than "global trade in oil" with annual profits, via rough estimate that by 2009 alone, being between US$400-500 billion, representing a significant percentage of illicit financial flow worldwide, between 2-5% global GDP.[263] Such numbers to the present, given the illicit nature of associated business and offshore accounts utilized for transfer of monetary assets from sales and distribution, are

---

[258] Ibid..

[259] Saab, Bilal Y., and Alexandra W. Taylor. "Criminality and Armed Groups: A Comparative Study of FARC and Paramilitary Groups in Colombia." *Studies in Conflict & Terrorism* 32, no. 6 (2009), 455-475. doi:10.1080/10576100902892570, p. 462.

[260] Ibid..

[261] Ibid..

[262] Ibid., p. 467.

[263] Ibid., p. 456.

inordinately hard to come by, and even such efforts as the journalistic consortium publishing the Panama Papers are still yielding results, including in Colombia and other areas of illicit trade.[264]

Critical Nexus: The ELN in Colombia and Venezuela

Colombia and Venezuela have a connected history; both were originally part of the short-lived republic made up of present-day Panama, Ecuador, Colombia, and Venezuela established by Simon Bolivar as Gran Colombia. While this state did not last, the connections among them remain indelible, while contentious, and even viciously violent depending upon the current political landscape. As of April 11, 2019, according to InsightCrime, Venezuela had "positioned 17 military bases along its border with Colombia in an effort to address what security officials describe as multiple attacks coming from Colombian paramilitary groups".[265] This has been, according to Venezuelan officials, because of "multiple aggressions from Iván Duque's narco-government"[266]. Such sentiments coming from the Maduro administration in Venezuela are not a surprise; Maduro is indeed a successor of Hugo Chavez and his own, stark iteration of a "Bolivarian Revolution".[267] Rather than declaring independence from Spain, the revolution Chavez sought to instigate was against "foreign (U.S.)-dominated political and economic systems in the Americas, to take power, and to create a socialist, nationalistic, and "popular"

---

[264] ICIJ. "The Panama Papers: Exposing the Rogue Offshore Finance Industry." ICIJ. Last modified August 3, 2018.
https://www.icij.org/investigations/panama-papers/.
[265] "Venezuela Govt Claims Military Buildup at Colombian Border is to Combat Criminal Groups." InSight Crime. Last modified April 12, 2019.
https://www.insightcrime.org/news/brief/venezuela-colombia-border-military-criminal-groups/.
[266] Ibid..
[267] Manwaring, Max G. Report. Strategic Studies Institute, US Army War College, 2012. http://www.jstor.org/stable/resrep11897, p. ix.

(direct) democracy in Venezuela" that would sooner or later extend throughout the Western Hemisphere.[268] The prevailing thought: that the "North American (U.S.) 'Empire' and its bourgeois political friends in Latin America are not doing what is right for the people, and that socialist Bolivarian philosophy and leadership will."[269] According to Manwaring, Latin America could only be such a revolutionary's "dream"—and Chavez was "prepared to help friends, partners, and allies to destabilize, to facilitate the processes of state failure, and to "destroy in order to build" in true revolutionary fashion."[270]

Incidentally, Chavez actively encouraged the idea of the Gen4 paradigm of asymmetric conflict to achieve this; he further encouraged his allies in Latin America, Russia, and Iran to support it, with the ultimate aim to "put an end to U.S. political and economic influence in the Western Hemisphere [ostensibly an anti-Monroe Doctrine] and transform the whole of Latin America into a single Bolivarian (Socialist) state."[271] Inherently, this would cause one dominant political form to transform into another, but first it would appear as "politicized militias, hegemonic non-state actors, and surrogates for traditional nation-states" would "move from war with some rules and conventions to new warmaking entities and into completely unrestricted warfare."[272] From that point, the failing and failed states would "evolve" to become new entities, wholly open to what would bring order, and Latin American *grandeza* could be realized.[273] This would be done via "three-front asymmetric war": 1) "agit-prop activities"; 2) "destabilization of the bourgeois enemy until his resolve is gone and the targeted

---

[268] Ibid..
[269] Ibid..
[270] Ibid., p. x.
[271] Ibid., p. 1.
[272] Ibid..
[273] Ibid..

country has reached failing or failed-state status"; and 3) "generating a force-multiplier by building alliances, partnerships, and coalitions."[274]

This would also involve "new roles" of "Bolivarian Popular Militias" in six phases—as espoused by General Gustavo Reyes Rangel Briceno in 2007—to achieve the "Marxian reward of history"—"liberation of Latin America from the U.S. political-economic hegemon".[275] These were (and I have shortened this for clarity/brevity):

- *Phase One*: Destabilization of targeted societies through the exploitation of a combination of four types of war-working within a general resistance: 1) temporal (prolonged) war; 2) creating chaos and instability; 3) economic war; and 4) media war;
- *Phase Two*: Create a popular (political front) out of the debourgeoised middle classes to compete with and weaken a targeted government;
- Phase Three: Foment regional conflicts involving "seeding operations" in developing and nurturing popular support for the war of resistance and establish "liberated zones" (quasi-states) within the state;
- *Phase Four*: Plan and implement overt and direct intimidation activities among the populace (demonstrations, strikes, civil violence, personal violence, murder) against feudal. Capitalistic, militaristic opponents and *yanqui* imperialism;
- *Phase Five:* Increase covert and overt political-psychological-economic-military actions to develop local popular militias to fight in their

---

[274] Ibid., p. 16.
[275] Ibid., p. 17.

own zones and coordinate with other local and district militias;

- *Phase Six:* Directly, but gradually, confront a demoralized enemy military force and bring about its desired collapse—or militarily invade a failing or failed state, compelling socialist governance.[276]

For Chavez and Briceno, this would be a process; essential to the process were what they considered a "'new' force multiplier" in terms of "alliances, partnerships, and coalitions" including "state and non-state actors and criminal-terrorist organizations": a South American/ Caribbean "Bolivarian" alliance, Iran and Russia, and such insurgencies/terrorists as (at the time) FARC, Hezbollah, and "other violent nonstate actors" such as Mexican Transnational Criminal Organizations (TCOs).[277] It would work economically as well as politically, for TCO's and state/state-sponsored terrorist organizations could "circumvent financial sanctions imposed by the United States, the European Union (EU), and the United Nations (UN) through access to the Venezuelan financial system" which would be especially attractive for a state like Iran, and its proxy, Hezbollah.[278]

The same could be said for illicit financing from Russia, as Russia was already delivering weapons to Venezuela, which included, by 2012, "24 combat aircraft, 44 attack helicopters, and 2,272 missiles and missile launchers" while also signing agreements for additional arms and training that amounted to over US$15 billion.[279] Manwaring completes his analysis of the "Chavez" plan by reminding

---

[276] Ibid., p.p. 18-19.
[277] Ibid., p.p. 22-23.
[278] Ibid., p. 25.
[279] Ibid., p. 28.

the reader that "protracted asymmetric war (4GW) is the only kind of conflict that a modern power has ever lost" and that it as of the date of his assessment in December 2012, "it is surprising and dismaying that the world's only superpower does not have a unified long-term strategy and a multidimensional interagency organizational architecture to deal with Chavez's 21st Century Socialism and its associated asymmetric war".[280]

Per Manwaring, this is the macrocosm which involves not just Venezuela, but a larger international involvement that taps directly into an asymmetric, criminal/terrorist vortex that if left unchecked—including because of hubris or distraction—would become an international security nightmare. On the more micro level, and in terms of regional instability, Chavez, and now Maduro, has only been playing into this playbook, seemingly to the letter, not only seeking to destroy the current systems in its own part of Latin America, but involving, as was predicted and predicated, Russia, Iran, and now China. And instead of counting on FARC because of the peace agreement, by 2016, it was apparent that the Venezuelans should look more directly to the remaining primary combatant assailing Colombia: the ELN.

Both Chavez, and Maduro after him, have given the ELN safe haven and support for operations;[281] in a 2008 address to parliament, Chavez legitimized the ELN (and at the time FARC) as a "genuine" army and an insurgent force "with a political goal".[282] InsightCrime has called them a Colombo-Venezuelan Rebel army," while ICG's Phil Gunson has suggested that on the Venezuelan side of the

---

[280280] Ibid., p. 33.
[281] "Gold and Grief in Venezuela's Violent South." Crisis Group. Last modified February 28, 2019. https://www.crisisgroup.org/latin-america-caribbean/andes/venezuela/073-gold-and-grief-venezuelas-violent-south, p.6
[282] Ibid..

border, the ELN "is more and more a Venezuelan organization, not Colombian, in the sense that its most important bases and its principal sources of income are on this side, where it recruits more and more Venezuelans."[283] While the ELN had been crossing over the border for decades, the ICG estimated that it is now present in 13 of 24 Venezuelan states, where it "controls radio stations, influences school curriculums and is closely connected to local politicians."[284] One NGO director confirmed that the ELN are not solely "border guerrillas" and "[t]hough they have camps throughout the border region, their activity in Venezuela is nationwide."[285]

With oil reserves and refining compromised, Maduro stepped up exploiting other sources of revenue, and while announcing US$5.5 billion in mining deals for 2016, claimed in 2018 during a UN General Assembly address that Venezuela had "potentially the world's largest gold reserves".[286] ICG estimated at the time that 60% of the ELN's income had been earned from illicit gold and other mining or "mining-related activities" (other resources include coltan, uranium, and diamonds), including charging a "tax" on illicit miners' earnings; on May 20, 2018, the day of the Presidential election in Venezuela, the ELN "reportedly seized a large number of mines" while people were in line to vote.[287] ICG also reported (as has InsightCrime), on operations along the border with Guyana and Brazil, with some having reported actual presences inside the borders themselves,[288] while one former ELN

---

[283] "Op-Ed: The ELN As a Colombo-Venezuelan Rebel Army." InSight Crime. Last modified March 25, 2019. https://www.insightcrime.org/news/analysis/op-ed-the-eln-as-a-colombo-venezuelan-rebel-army/.
[284] ICG, "Gold and Grief," p. 6.
[285] Ibid..
[286] Ibid., p. 4.
[287] Ibid..
[288] Ibid., p. 7.

official had suggested they had been inside these borders for over 10 years.[289]

Also in these areas, the ELN also operates a veritable laundry list of activity and "allegedly engages in cattle smuggling, gasoline smuggling, extortion, food distribution, recruitment of minors, attacks on security officials" and what Command and the older guard specifically and officially have always prohibited: drug trafficking,[290] while others insist that drugs are still considered anathema; "drugs and alcohol are prohibited in mines under guerrilla control"[291] and in ELN-controlled communities, where it has ostensibly taken on the role of the state, "[a]lcohol and drug consumption are not tolerated and punishable by death."[292]

The border between Venezuela and Colombia has also now presented a distinct uptick in illicit activity, given the mass exodus of Venezuelans into Colombia across different points along its 1,300 mile border; over 2 million Venezuelans have migrated to Colombia (where they are not considered by the Colombian government refugees), up to 32,000 per day as of 2018,[293] with the estimates being that it would reach four million by 2020[294]—numbers which are currently still being determined. Because the border at different points had been officially closed between Colombia and Venezuela, the ELN and other groups nevertheless operated 78 or more illegal trails, *trochas,* charging, as last reported, from 20,000 bolivars, or US$7,

---

[289] Ibid..

[290] "ELN Now Present in Half of Venezuela." InSight Crime. Last modified November 15, 2018. https://www.insightcrime.org/news/analysis/eln-present-half-venezuela/.

[291] ICG, "Gold and Grief," p. 8.

[292] Ibid., p. 15.

[293] "Responding to an Exodus: Venezuela's Migration Crisis." WOLA. Last modified August 2, 2018. https://www.wola.org/2018/07/responding-exodus-venezuelas-migration-refugee-crisis-seen-colombian-brazilian-borders/.

[294] Ibid., p. 14.

which exceeds a monthly Venezuelan salary[295] to up to US$100, depending upon whether its for migration, or for illicit smuggling.[296] Such *trochas*, some have reported, also used for human smuggling; women and children can be trafficked to be sold or to be used as sex workers in Cucuta, Colombia, while small children on the *trochas* themselves are often utilized for "intelligence" or to "transport fuel".[297] Small arms are also brought across the border, bought cheaply in Venezuela for COP$400,000 (US$140) and sold for COP$1.3 million (US$470). The crisis in Venezuela has also caused Venezuelans themselves to join the ELN ranks, where they are housed, fed, indoctrinated, and also paid, receiving 50,000 (US$300) bolivars per month, more that 27 times the minimum Venezuelan wage.[298]

In recalling Manwaring and his caution about the longer-term plan for Venezuela, and with the Venezuelan government long having been direct support for the ELN, a mutual interest in a larger "Bolivarian" state is perhaps slowly being realized, and according to the strategies and tactics described. Adding to the mix are the presences of both Cuba and China in Venezuela; the Chinese Development Bank had "provided more than $30 billion in loans tied to oil production" and had, by 2019, sold more than $615 million in weapons to the Venezuelan

---

[295] "Trails Along Colombia-Venezuela Border Are Criminal Enclaves." InSight Crime. Last modified March 19, 2019. https://www.insightcrime.org/news/brief/trochas-colombia-venezuela-criminal-enclave/.

[296] United Nations High Commissioner for Refugees. "As Colombia Tightens Its Border, More Venezuelan Migrants Brave Clandestine Routes." Refworld. Last modified April 10, 2019. https://www.refworld.org/docid/5b7400ef0.html.

[297] Ibid.

[298] "Colombia's ELN, Ex-FARC Mafia Recruiting Hungry Venezuela Migrants." InSight Crime. Last modified October 16, 2018. https://www.insightcrime.org/news/brief/colombias-eln-ex-farc-mafia-recruiting-hungry-venezuela-migrants/.

government.[299] It has additionally developed, via ZTE, an ID card to "monitor citizens' behavior".[300] On April 10, 2019, Raul Castro of Cuba, in a speech to the Cuban Communist Party National Assembly, announced Cuba's continued support of Venezuela, while U.S. Vice President Mike Pence, before the UN Security Council that the U.S. "would announce…action to hold Cuba accountable for its support of Venezuela's president Nicolas Maduro" while accusing "Cuban security and intelligence officials of propping up Maduro's government".[301]

This is also while Iran had been a continuing active presence; it has ostensibly been "doubling down" on their support for Maduro,[302] including bringing in direct flights between Tehran and Caracas.[303] While some believed this has been a means of testing the U.S., who had backed Maduro's challenger, Juan Guiado, considering him the legitimate leader, the Iranian presence has been more insidious in the past. Iran's proxy, Hezbollah, has long been known to operate "active cells" in Venezuela, including activity in the nefarious location off the coast of Venezuela, Margarita Island, where it has had a presence for some

---

[299] Seligman, Lara. "U.S. Military Wary of China's Foothold in Venezuela." Foreign Policy. Last modified April 8, 2019. https://foreignpolicy.com/2019/04/08/us-military-wary-of-chinas-foothold-in-venezuela-maduro-faller-guaido-trump-pentagon/.

[300] Ibid..

[301] "Raúl Castro Pledges Cuba Will Never Abandon Venezuela." The Guardian. Last modified April 11, 2019. https://www.theguardian.com/world/2019/apr/10/raul-castro-cuba-never-abandon-venezuela?CMP=twt_a-world_b-gdnworld.

[302] "Bloomberg." Bloomberg - Are You a Robot?. Accessed April 13, 2019. https://www.bloomberg.com/news/articles/2019-02-01/iran-slams-u-s-over-venezuela-secretly-some-may-be-relieved.

[303] "Iranian Delegation Travels to Venezuela to Discuss Direct Flight Route." U.S. Last modified April 8, 2019. https://www.reuters.com/article/us-iran-venezuela-airlines/irans-mahan-air-launches-direct-flights-to-venezuela-idUSKCN1RK1VM.

time.[304] This is in addition to the Tri-Border region of Argentina, Brazil, and Paraguay, where terrorist training camps and other illicit activity, including terrorist cells in operation, have existed since the end of the Cold War. Additionally, the narco-terrorist connection has been well established in Venezuela, including via Chekry Harb, "a drug trafficker and money laundering kingpin," *nomme de guerre* "Taliban," who according to *Foreign Policy*:

> …used Panama and Venezuela as critical hubs in an operation that sent narcotics from Colombia to the United States, West Africa, the Middle East, and Europe. Proceeds from the cocaine-trafficking ring were laundered into Colombian pesos or Venezuelan bolivars, with Hezbollah netting between 8 and 14 percent of profits.[305]

Indeed, the ELN is a part of this nexus, and the larger implications are yet to be determined. However, depending upon how deeply the United States wants to dive into the Venezuelan crisis—including now under the Biden administration, those affected: 33 million people, spread across twice the territory of Iraq, with 160,000 regular military and insurgents, *colectivos*, and other armed criminal contingents numbering up to 100,000,[306] including the ELN, with over 50 years of insurgent experience, deeply entrenched in Venezuela, Colombia, and again with presences in Guyana, Brazil, Suriname, and Ecuador. And in

---

[304] Clarke, Colin P. "Hezbollah Is in Venezuela to Stay." Foreign Policy. Last modified February 9, 2019. https://foreignpolicy.com/2019/02/09/hezbollah-is-in-venezuela-to-stay/.
[305] Ibid..
[306] "What a Military Intervention in Venezuela Would Look Like." Foreign Affairs. Last modified March 26, 2019. https://www.foreignaffairs.com/articles/venezuela/2019-03-19/what-military-intervention-venezuela-would-look.

such a case as any intervention is conceived, there is the distinct possibility that the U.S. may indeed adopt the usual rhetoric and operational tenor of superpower, including in RAND-style hyper-intellectualism, rather than paying any attention to the realities on the ground. That includes millions of Venezuelans in crisis, affecting all of the countries along Venezuelan borders, especially Colombia where routes are already established.

Unfortunately, too, this in the past has also directly played into Maduro's hands (especially during the Trump administration), should he choose to continue following the Chavez "Bolivarian" playbook; any such direct—especially military—intervention at any point would smack directly of the imperialist image Chavez wanted to promote, and it would, should any U.S. administration purport to do so for "humanitarian reasons" be met with more than reasonable skepticism. As Halliday so aptly put it in 1999, "don't invade a revolution."[307] But more than that, there is an acute danger in the imposition of outside will upon any population, as Colombia can prove by virtue of decades of its own insurgencies.

As Samuel Huntington warned regarding Western developed hegemony, such hegemony, or belief in its indelible presence, can also be accompanied by inordinate hubris.[308] Our ways are not to be foisted upon others, no matter our interests, particularly solipsistic, should we want to preserve our own legitimacy. The world in this information age, and given the complexities of increased developing world conflict and populism in both the developed and developing world, our belief that "Western institutions, values, and culture constitute 'the highest, most enlightened, most liberal, most rational, most modern, and

---

[307] Goldstone, p. 145.
[308] Simons, p. 400.

most civilized thinking of humankind'" can be, especially when thinking about the current political mire in which the United States finds itself, "false, immoral, and dangerous."[309] We have had to deal with our own non-state terrorism—if not nascent insurgency—over the last years, including challenges to the Constitution and rule of law in a self-interested, alternate-reality populist uprising exemplified by invasion of the U.S. Capitol building on January 6, 2021. The message: no state in this day and age can take its own security for granted. With this in mind, we need to remember that every state has its own complexities that we ignore to our peril—including that of the state in which we seek to intervene.

---

[309] Ibid..

Bibliography

Alvira, Gustavo. "Toward a New Amnesty: The Colombian Peace Process and the Inter-American Court of Human Rights." *Tulane Journal of International and Comparative Law* 22 (2013), 119-144. https://heinonline.org.

Amnesty International Home. Accessed April 5, 2019. http://www.amnesty.org.

Andrade, Luis M. "Liberation Theology: A Critique of Modernity." *Interventions* 19, no. 5 (2017), 620-630. doi:10.1080/1369801x.2017.1336461.

"As Peace Talks Flail, Colombia's ELN Seeks 'Liberation or Death'." InSight Crime. Last modified October 10, 2018. https://www.insightcrime.org/news/analysis/peace-talks-flail-colombias-eln-seeks-liberation-death/.

"Bloomberg." Bloomberg – "Iran Slams U.S. Over Venezuela." Accessed April 13, 2019. https://www.bloomberg.com/news/articles/2019-02-01/iran-slams-u-s-over-venezuela-secretly-some-may-be-relieved.

Bouvier, Virginia M. *Colombia: Building Peace in a Time of War*. US Institute of Peace Press, 2009.

"Briefing: Needs Mount in Colombia As Peace Commitments Lag." The New Humanitarian. Last modified April 4, 2019. https://www.thenewhumanitarian.org/analysis/2019/03/25/briefing-needs-mount-colombia-peace-commitments-lag.

Bunker, Robert. *Old and New Insurgency Forms*. Perennial Press, 2018.

Casa Editorial El Tiempo. "Colombia, 40 Años Atrapada En El Negocio Del Tráfico De Cocaína." El Tiempo. Last modified April 11, 2019. https://www.eltiempo.com/justicia/conflicto-y-narcotrafico/como-ha-sido-el-negocio-del-trafico-de-coca-en-colombia-348756.

Clarke, Colin P. "Hezbollah Is in Venezuela to Stay." Foreign Policy. Last modified February 9, 2019. https://foreignpolicy.com/2019/02/09/hezbollah-is-in-venezuela-to-stay/.

Clausewitz, Carl V. *On War*. 1908.

"Colombia President Duque's 5 'Hot Potatoes'." InSight Crime. Last modified
    August 8, 2018.
    https://www.insightcrime.org/news/analysis/colombia-president-
    duque-5-hot-potatoes/.

"Colombia: Background and U.S. Relations." Congressional Research Service.
    Last modified February 8, 2019.
    https://fas.org/sgp/crs/row/R43813.pdf.

"Colombian President-elect Ivan Duque Visits U.S. Southern Command." U.S.
    Southern Command. Last modified July 14, 2018.
    https://www.southcom.mil/MEDIA/NEWS-
    ARTICLES/Article/1575023/colombian-president-elect-ivan-duque-
    visits-us-southern-command/.

"Colombia's ELN Rebel Leaders Say They Will Not Leave Cuba." U.S. Last
    modified January 31, 2019. https://www.reuters.com/article/us-
    colombia-rebels/colombias-eln-rebel-leaders-say-they-will-not-leave-
    cuba-idUSKCN1PP2V5.

"Colombia's ELN, Ex-FARC Mafia Recruiting Hungry Venezuela Migrants."
    InSight Crime. Last modified October 16, 2018.
    https://www.insightcrime.org/news/brief/colombias-eln-ex-farc-
    mafia-recruiting-hungry-venezuela-migrants/.

"Colombia's President Iván Duque Undermines a Peace Deal." The
    Economist. Last modified March 14, 2019.
    https://www.economist.com/the-americas/2019/03/14/colombias-
    president-ivan-duque-undermines-a-peace-deal.

Daase, Christopher. "Clausewitz and Small Wars." *Clausewitz in the Twenty-
    First Century*, 2007, 182-195.
    doi:10.1093/acprof:oso/9780199232024.003.0011.

Davies, James C. "Toward a Theory of Revolution." *American Sociological
    Review* 27, no. 1 (1962), 5. doi:10.2307/2089714.

Echevarria II, Antulio J. "Fourth-Generation War and Other Myths." *Strategic
    Studies Institute*, November 2008, i. - 21.
    https://ssi.armywarcollege.edu/pdffiles/PUB632.pdf.

"ELN Now Present in Half of Venezuela." InSight Crime. Last modified
    November 15, 2018.
    https://www.insightcrime.org/news/analysis/eln-present-half-
    venezuela/.

"The ELN's Attack on the National Police Academy in Bogotá and Its
    Implications – Combating Terrorism Center at West Point."

Combating Terrorism Center at West Point. Last modified March 4, 2019. https://ctc.usma.edu/elns-attack-national-police-academy-bogota-implications/.

Federation Of American Scientists – Science for a Safer, More Informed World. Accessed March 28, 2019. https://fas.org/sgp/crs/misc/R42575.pdf.

"Field Listing :: Refugees and Internally Displaced Persons — The World Factbook." Welcome to the CIA Web Site — Central Intelligence Agency. Accessed April 8, 2019. https://www.cia.gov/library/publications/the-world-factbook/fields/327.html.

"FRONTLINE/WORLD . Colombia - The Pipeline War . Global Reach: U.S. Corporate Interests in Columbia | PBS." PBS: Public Broadcasting Service. Accessed April 8, 2019. http://www.pbs.org/frontlineworld/stories/colombia/corporate.html.

"Gold and Grief in Venezuela's Violent South." Crisis Group. Last modified February 28, 2019. https://www.crisisgroup.org/latin-america-caribbean/andes/venezuela/073-gold-and-grief-venezuelas-violent-south.

Goldstone, Jack A. "Toward a Fourth Generation of Revolutionary Theory." *SSRN Electronic Journal*, 2001. doi:10.2139/ssrn.1531902.

Gramer, Robbie and Johnson, Keith. "Tillerson Praises Monroe Doctrine, Warns Latin America of 'Imperial? Chinese Ambitions." Foreign Policy. Last modified February 2, 2018. https://foreignpolicy.com/2018/02/02/tillerson-praises-monroe-doctrine-warns-latin-america-off-imperial-chinese-ambitions-mexico-south-america-nafta-diplomacy-trump-trade-venezuela-maduro/.

Guevara, Ernesto. *Che Guevara on Guerrilla Warfare*. New York: Praeger, 1961.

Guevara, Ernesto C. *Reminiscences of the Cuban Revolutionary War: Authorized Edition*. Sussex: Ocean Press, 2012.

Harris, Richard L. "Cuban Internationalism, Che Guevara, and the Survival of Cuba's Socialist Regime." *Latin American Perspectives* 36, no. 3 (2009), 27-42. doi:10.1177/0094582x09334165.

Hoskin, Gary, and Richard Maullin. "Soldiers, Guerrillas and Politics in Colombia." *The American Political Science Review* 71, no. 1 (1977),

389. doi:10.2307/1957041.

Hylton, Forrest. "The Experience of Defeat." *Historical Materialism* 22, no. 1
(2014), 67-104. doi:10.1163/1569206x-12341335.

ICIJ. "The Panama Papers: Exposing the Rogue Offshore Finance Industry."
ICIJ. Last modified August 3, 2018.
https://www.icij.org/investigations/panama-papers/.

International Committee of the Red Cross. Accessed May 8, 2019.
https://www.icrc.org/en/download/file/13953/irrc-882-codes-
conduct.pdf.

"Iranian Delegation Travels to Venezuela to Discuss Direct Flight Route."
U.S. Last modified April 8, 2019.
https://www.reuters.com/article/us-iran-venezuela-airlines/irans-
mahan-air-launches-direct-flights-to-venezuela-idUSKCN1RK1VM.
Kalyvas, Stathis N. *The Logic of Violence in Civil War*. Cambridge: Cambridge
University Press, 2006.

Kaplan, Stephen B., and Michael Penfold. "China and Russia have deep
financial ties to Venezuela. Here's what's at stake." The Washington
Post. Last modified February 22, 2019.
https://www.washingtonpost.com/politics/2019/02/22/china-russia-
have-deep-financial-ties-venezuela-heres-whats-
stake/?utm_term=.8c0042e10196.

Kleinfeld, Rachel, and Robert Muggah. "The State of War." Carnegie
Endowment for International Peace. Last modified March 18, 2019.
https://carnegieendowment.org/2019/03/18/state-of-war-pub-78630.

Kronenberg, Clive W. "Manifestations of Humanism in Revolutionary
Cuba." *Latin American Perspectives* 36, no. 2 (2009), 66-80.
doi:10.1177/0094582x09331953.

Lind, William S. "Understanding Fourth Generation War." *Military Review*,
September/October 2004, 12-16.

Long, Austin. "What are insurgencies and how does one fight them?" In *On
"Other War": Lessons from Five Decades of RAND
Counterinsurgency Research*, 21-32. Santa Monica: Rand
Corporation, 2006.

Mackin, Robert S. "Liberation Theology: The Radicalization of Social
Catholic Movements." *Politics, Religion & Ideology* 13, no. 3
(2012), 333-351. doi:10.1080/21567689.2012.698979.

Manwaring, Max G. "Nonstate Actors in Colombia: Threat and Response."
    Strategic Studies Institute (SSI) | US Army War College. Accessed
    April 8, 2019.
    https://ssi.armywarcollege.edu/pubs/display.cfm?pubID=16.

McKenzie, Jr., Kenneth F. "Elegant irrelevance: fourth-generation
    warfare." *Parameters*, Fall 1993, 51-60.

McLaren, Peter, and Petar Jandrić. "Karl Marx and Liberation Theology:
    Dialectical Materialism and Christian Spirituality in, against, and
    beyond Contemporary Capitalism." *tripleC: Communication,
    Capitalism & Critique. Open Access Journal for a Global
    Sustainable Information Society* 16, no. 2 (2018), 598-607.
    doi:10.31269/triplec.v16i2.965.

Mehraj, Hakim Khalid, Akhtar Neyaz Bhat, and Hakeem Rameez Mehraj.
    "Impacts OF Media on Society: A Sociological
    Perspective." *International Journal of Humanities and Social
    Science Invention* 3, no. 6 (June 2014), 56-64.
    http://www.ijhssi.org/papers/v3(6)/Version-4/L0364056064.pdf.

"The Missing Peace: Colombia's New Government and Last Guerrillas."
    Crisis Group. Last modified July 12, 2018.
    https://www.crisisgroup.org/latin-america-
    caribbean/andes/colombia/68-missing-peace-colombias-new-
    government-and-last-guerrillas.

"Nation State: A Glossary of Political Economy Terms - Dr. Paul M.
    Johnson." Auburn University. Accessed April 10, 2019.
    http://www.auburn.edu/~johnspm/gloss/nation_state.

"Neocolonialism." Encyclopedia Britannica. Accessed April 9, 2019.
    https://www.britannica.com/topic/neocolonialism.

"The Nobel Peace Prize 2016." NobelPrize.org. Accessed April 12, 2019.
    https://www.nobelprize.org/prizes/peace/2016/santos/facts/.

"Op-Ed: The ELN As a Colombo-Venezuelan Rebel Army." InSight Crime.
    Last modified March 25, 2019.
    https://www.insightcrime.org/news/analysis/op-ed-the-eln-as-a-
    colombo-venezuelan-rebel-army/.

Popkin, Samuel L. *The Rational Peasant: The Political Economy of Rural
    Society in Vietnam*. Oakland: University of California Press, 1979.

"Raúl Castro Pledges Cuba Will Never Abandon Venezuela." The Guardian.
    Last modified April 10, 2019.

https://www.theguardian.com/world/2019/apr/10/raul-castro-cuba-
never-abandon-venezuela?CMP=twt_a-world_b-gdnworld.

"Raúl Castro Pledges Cuba Will Never Abandon Venezuela." The Guardian.
Last modified April 11, 2019.
https://www.theguardian.com/world/2019/apr/10/raul-castro-cuba-
never-abandon-venezuela?CMP=twt_a-world_b-gdnworld.

"Responding to an Exodus: Venezuela's Migration Crisis." WOLA. Last
modified August 2, 2018.
https://www.wola.org/2018/07/responding-exodus-venezuelas-
migration-refugee-crisis-seen-colombian-brazilian-borders/.

Saab, Bilal Y., and Alexandra W. Taylor. "Criminality and Armed Groups: A
Comparative Study of FARC and Paramilitary Groups in
Colombia." *Studies in Conflict & Terrorism* 32, no. 6 (2009), 455-
475. doi:10.1080/10576100902892570.

Seligman, Lara. "U.S. Military Wary of China's Foothold in Venezuela."
Foreign Policy. Last modified April 8, 2019.
https://foreignpolicy.com/2019/04/08/us-military-wary-of-chinas-
foothold-in-venezuela-maduro-faller-guaido-trump-pentagon/.

Simons, G. "Fourth Generation Warfare and The Clash of
Civilizations." *Journal of Islamic Studies* 21, no. 3 (2010), 391-412.
doi:10.1093/jis/etq042.

Skocpol, Theda. "What makes peasants revolutionary?" *Social revolutions in
the modern world*(n.d.), 213-239.
doi:10.1017/cbo9781139173834.010.

Staniland, Paul. *Networks of Rebellion: Explaining Insurgent Cohesion and
Collapse*. Ithaca: Cornell University Press, 2014.

"TEACHING THE CLAUSEWITZIAN TRINITY." Carl Von Clausewitz
Resources. Accessed April 10, 2019.
https://www.clausewitz.com/readings/Bassford/Trinity/TrinityTeach
ingNote.htm.

Thornton, Rod. *Asymmetric Warfare: Threat and Response in the 21st
Century*. Cambridge: Polity, 2007.

Tompkins, Jr., Paul J., and Summer Newton. "Case Studies in Insurgency and
Revolutionary Warfare - Colombia (1964-2009)." United States
Army Special Operations Command. Accessed April 9, 2019.
http://www.soc.mil/ARIS/ARIS_Colombia-BOOK.pdf.

"Trails Along Colombia-Venezuela Border Are Criminal Enclaves." InSight
    Crime. Last modified March 19, 2019.
    https://www.insightcrime.org/news/brief/trochas-colombia-
    venezuela-criminal-enclave/.

Tse-tung, Mao. *On Guerrilla Warfare.* North Chelmsford: Courier
    Corporation, 2012.

United Nations High Commissioner for Refugees. "As Colombia Tightens Its
    Border, More Venezuelan Migrants Brave Clandestine Routes."
    Refworld. Last modified April 10, 2019.
    https://www.refworld.org/docid/5b7400ef0.html.

Vanden, Harry E. "Marxism and the Peasantry in Latin America:
    Marginalization or Mobilization?" *Latin American Perspectives* 9,
    no. 4 (1982), 74-98. doi:10.1177/0094582x8200900405.

"Venezuela Govt Claims Military Buildup at Colombian Border is to Combat
    Criminal Groups." InSight Crime. Last modified April 12, 2019.
    https://www.insightcrime.org/news/brief/venezuela-colombia-
    border-military-criminal-groups/.

Waldman, Thomas. "Politics and War: Clausewitz's Paradoxical
    Equation." *Parameters*, Fall 2010, 1-13.
    https://www.clausewitz.com/opencourseware/Waldman2.pdf.

"What a Military Intervention in Venezuela Would Look Like." Foreign
    Affairs. Last modified March 26, 2019.
    https://www.foreignaffairs.com/articles/venezuela/2019-03-19/what-
    military-intervention-venezuela-would-look.

"Why Colombians Distrust the FARC Peace Deal." The Economist. Last
    modified May 24, 2018. https://www.economist.com/the-economist-
    explains/2018/05/24/why-colombians-distrust-the-farc-peace-deal.

Author Biography

K.J. Wetherholt is a writer, academic, journalist, subject matter expert (SME) on modern war, and the Publisher/Executive Editor of MIPJ and Humanitas. Wetherholt's previous publications include a book about WWI, and she is currently researching several projects about war, heresy, and liberation and their impacts on humanity, past and present.

www.ingramcontent.com/pod-product-compliance
Lightning Source LLC
Chambersburg PA
CBHW052137090426
42741CB00009B/2120